Fleecing the Lambs

Fleecing the Lambs

by Christopher Elias

Henry Regnery Company • Chicago

To my wife, Alyne,
and to Christopher
and Caroline.

Contents

viii   *Contents*

Preface

You don't have to observe Wall Street for very long to realize that it is a world unlike any other—and not a very honest one. Wall Street is full of people, nearly all of whom are arrogant, some of whom are very rich, and some of whom according to the rules the average citizen must obey, very crooked. Most of them regard the average investor as a "sucker," useful only to generate commissions for his broker, who will sell him remnants of a new, shaky issue or a tired stock that the Street's firms or its principals are pitching. That's if they want the average investor's business at all.

The rules that govern the Street are written by Wall Streeters, for the reforms of the 1930s merely made Wall Street more cautious, not any less larcenous. Wall Streeters still act as if they are immune to common law even though their dishonesty is well documented, and the Exchange enforces its rules as it sees fit. As is the case with most self-regulating industries, its members are not all equal under the rules. As for the investor, the Exchange decides nothing that will give him an even break.

My own introduction to Wall Street came many years ago when I was a writer for *Business Week*. I was shocked to learn how an executive of Ira Haupt & Company used the funds of customers to gamble in the commodities market, naively accepting receipts for salad oil that didn't exist. The scandals at the American Stock Exchange, where it was discovered that a specialist bought shares for its president, were just as shocking. At the *Magazine of Wall Street,* I discovered that the policy of the publisher was to buy rewritten and very old work of analysts and to present it to the subscribers–investors as new and timely material. The analysts were paid $100 to be a party to this deception.

During that time, when I wrote a series of editorials against the "giveup," the practice whereby brokers split fees from institutions with anyone specified by the institutions, I received a telephone call from a surprised and indignant Manny Cohen, chairman of the SEC, who asked in wonderment, "Do you realize what you're doing?"

It seems that to pit oneself against the dishonest though accepted practices prevalent in the Street is to set out on a course hard for others to believe, if not downright dangerous. The anger of Robert Haack, president of the Exchange, was such that after I left the Exchange and offered to reproduce faithfully and in context anything he cared to say, he refused to acknowledge the invitation. It was hardly an unexpected response. But sullenness from the New York Stock Exchange is no answer to the shady practices of the Street. Those questionable practices have cost people everywhere billions of dollars.

What is shocking in Wall Street, too, is the absolute power of the Exchange over the people who earn their living there. That power is very clearly translated into fear. This book could not have been written without a great deal of help from people who work in Wall Street. Yet while scores of them said that the kind of book I planned needed to be written and many spoke freely, *not one* agreed to be identified. Even those who strongly believe major reform is needed asked not to be named. A director and officer of the Exchange who supplied me with many facts called me days after our meeting, apparently after giving what he had said a great deal of thought, and, in a voice that trembled, he asked me not to use what he had told me. He said that if I did make use of the information, he would have me fired from my job as editor of the Exchange magazine.

The executive of a major firm who met me for lunch long after I had been terminated asked me not to leave the restaurant with him. Though we were many blocks from Wall Street, he still feared being seen with me. The great fear of most of the people I talked to was not only that they might lose the jobs they currently had but that they would be blackballed from *any* kind of a job if they were acknowledged sources for *Fleecing the Lambs*.

No institution, including the government, has the right to instill that kind of fear in the people who serve it. Criticism aimed at honest reform should be the right of everyone. Only an institution with a great deal to hide would wield such a blackjack. And the Exchange has much to hide.

Yet that fear of identification was very real among my sources, and I am forced to acknowledge all those who did help me with an unspecified but sincere "thank you." The lone exception, as she knows, is Laura.

CHRISTOPHER ELIAS

NEW YORK
July 1, 1971.

Part 1

Fleecing the lambs

1

The poll

It is Monday morning on Wall Street. From Broadway to the East River, the Street is crowded with people hurrying to work. Many are from Brooklyn, the Bronx, and other places in New York where rents are low. They walk fast, dodging trucks that mount the sidewalks to park, and some are clearly irritable after riding in hot, crowded subways. Most are plainly dressed, often in clothes that need pressing.

It is a clear, fresh April day in 1970. Over the weekend the smog has cleared away, and the air is full of sunshine. On each side of Wall Street, the flags of various banks fly alongside of the stars and stripes, suggesting a gala scene. Here and there peddlers already have rolled pushcarts full of hot dogs and panty hose into position, close to the passing crowds. At the curbs the long black Cadillacs and snub-nosed Mercedes favored by Wall Streeters already are lining up.

At the small square formed by the meeting of Wall and

Broad Streets, a black man wearing a flopping army coat climbs the steps of the subtreasury building, where George Washington took his oath of office in 1789 and from which so many political and war speeches have been delivered. In the coming summer the streets in front of the building would be the site of fearsome beatings of young antiwar people by hard-hat construction workers. But on this Monday in April, the building serves only as a backdrop for the black man. He jumps to the pedestal supporting a fifteen-foot bronze statue of Washington and beneath its outstretched arm and extended stomach, begins a shuffling dance. Occasionally he stops to point at the passing crowd and curse. No one pays much attention, though, since the black man's dance is practically a ritual.

Across the street in the New York Stock Exchange building, the staff has been arriving since eight o'clock. On the sixth floor Robert W. Haack, the Exchange president, is already at his desk. At fifty-three years of age Haack is a well built six-footer. His hair is dark and barely touched by gray. When he smiles, which is often, he displays a great many good teeth; as a type he might easily be cast for a movie role as a naval officer, which is in fact what he was during World War II.

On this day in April, 1970, he looks every bit the part he must play as the securities industry's most visible leader. He is dressed in the rich but subdued Wall Street style, which requires a vest, although Haack frequently discards both jacket and vest when he is working alone or seeing subordinates. His immaculate grooming is heightened considerably by the never-fading tan evident even in midwinter. He is not considered a vain man by his associates, but Haack's hair always seems combed, and it is well understood in the public relations and advertising departments of the Exchange that no profile picture of Haack, whose Dutch nose is strong and jutting, is to be used either in the Exchange's advertising or in distributions to the press.

Haack came to the Exchange in 1967 after a tour as president of the over-the-counter market's regulating body—the National Association of Securities Dealers (NASD). His predecessor, G. Keith Funston, was a former college president who turned out to be an extraordinary tub thumper for Wall Street. In fact, in the history of the Street no one had ever been able to persuade Americans to buy stocks in quantities so great, and Funston's success went beyond every expectation, including his own. In 1959, for example, a study made by the Exchange's own research staff on Funston's orders projected a stock trading volume averaging 4.5 million shares a day by 1970. (At the same time, a projection of 6 million shares a day by an outside consultant was discarded as being much too high.) As it turned out, trading had accelerated to 12 to 15 million shares a day by 1969, with an occasional 20-million-share day turning up. Even in the bear market of late 1969 and 1970 the Exchange's average volume was 10 million shares a day. Then, in 1971, with a market recovery underway, 20-million-share days became common.

The number of shareholders likewise increased enormously during Funston's term. When he arrived in Wall Street, 5 million people owned stocks directly. When he left, the number had increased to 22 million. In addition, over 100 million people in the United States had invested indirectly in the market by allocating parts of their salaries to pension plans, by buying mutual funds, or by investing in savings investment plans where they worked. By 1971, four years after Haack had succeeded Funston, the number of Americans owning stock directly had risen to 40 million, and no one could really say for sure how much of the population owned shares indirectly. The only thing certain was that the number was much higher than that of the direct owners.

If all the money Wall Streeters made out of this bonanza had been converted to dollar bills and spread out on the Street, they literally could have wallowed in their gains. Wall Street, in fact, had never been so flush, not even in the heady days of the 1920s.

Unfortunately, at the same time its firms had never been so greedy, nor its leaders so incompetent, shortsighted, and even dishonest.

Most Wall Street brokerage firms still are partnerships or privately held corporations owned by relatively few people.

This means there is no requirement for a public accounting, as in the case of stockholder-owned corporations. Income, costs, profits, the use of customers' funds, and every other pertinent financial fact are secrets so well kept that even the Securities and Exchange Commission (SEC) and the Exchange itself have trouble getting hold of the books.

But it hardly requires a look at the books or the balance sheet to tell what Wall Street's successful firms were up to during those days of the late 1960s. Much of the money that was made went into the pockets of the partners, who carried it home to Park Avenue, Connecticut, Westchester County, Mountain Lakes, and Morristown. The cash went to buy lavish estates and second homes. It bought yachts that sometimes never left their docks and sleek racing sailboats that never raced. It rented villas in Europe and Mexico and took Wall Streeters on grouse hunts in Scotland. It took some of them into Brooks Brothers to upgrade their wardrobes and others to galleries to indulge their tastes. A few embarked on safaris or to resorts in Africa, where they sat on a hotel balcony, drinks in hand, watching animals appear at a nearby watering hole each evening. The booty made sports car buffs or car collectors of some, and many a Riley, Morgan, and ancient Cord was paid for with money made in the Street. A great many men, still preferring conventional elegance, bought Rolls-Royces, Mercedes, and Cadillacs—or one of each. A few men close to Richard Nixon before he became president contributed to his classic political campaign and a number of Wall Streeters bought condominium apartments in Florida's Del Ray Beach, in anticipation of Nixon's part-time residency there.

Of course not all the money made on the Street was spent for pleasure or self-aggrandizement. Some was put into Swiss bank accounts and some into run-of-the-mill (tax-free) municipal bonds and Treasury bills. Some was even put into Black Angus cattle to acquire a tax loss, and some was put into oil exploration—which also became a tax loss if the result was only dry wells.

Very little money was put back, however, into the brokerage

firms. When it was, it was done with shortsightedness hard to believe, for the rule seemed to be that every dollar spent had to bring in many many more. It was the kind of thinking expected of men who still ran their businesses out of their hats, and as such they made the mistakes such men would make.

Greedily, the Street moguls opened boardrooms everywhere and hired about anyone to staff them as salesmen. They advertised heavily and installed expensive computers to pick stocks and print out analyses at the touch of a button. With an eye on the lush institutional market of mutual funds, banks, college endowments, pension funds, insurance companies, and other big traders, all of which were committed to "go-go" trading, the partners poured money into departments that could trade large blocks. They also published lengthy stock studies, containing more trivia than pertinent fact, to impress the institutions with research that was heavy but far from weighty.

All the while they were undermining their own capital base. In the manner of the odd-lot, crap-shooting stock buyer whom they professed to despise, the partners of many firms were buying the most speculative stocks imaginable and making them a part of their firms' capital structures. Indeed, some firms added stocks that were issued privately by corporations so new and untried that their securities could not be traded publicly.

It made no difference that the back offices of more than fifty firms—among them Hayden, Stone, Goodbody & Company, and McDonnell & Company—were breaking down under the paperwork load generated by the massive trading volume. Nor did anyone in the front office, with just a few exceptions—the most noteworthy being Merrill Lynch—believe for years that there was any need to put money into those back offices, though salaries were so low and conditions so bad there that only people with marginal education and intelligence cared to work in them.

Only in 1969 did the firms begin to inject money and management into the back office. And by then it was too late. The back office system itself, referred to as the cage, could not respond since it had been developed in the late 1890s and was geared to handle the low volume of another century. Though computers used elsewhere in the firms were able to turn out morning lines of hot stocks in seconds, clerks in the cage still needed hours to shuffle papers, including the actual stock cer- tificates required to complete transactions. In 1968 the cage broke down so completely throughout Wall Street that the firms could not even deliver securities to each other, much less to their customers. Thus, between "fails" to deliver stocks among themselves and continued massive trading volume, the back offices simply stopped operating.

The effect of this collapse on the individual investor was widespread. Not infrequently he was sent the wrong stock; when he was sent the right certificate, it arrived late. Often he would not receive it at all. If he left his stock in a Street name—with his broker—there was a good chance he would never receive his dividends—a certain sign that there was no record of owner- ship at his broker's office. If he left cash with the firm in safe- keeping (drawing no interest), the brokerage firm, whether sound or near bankruptcy, used it to buy many a shaky stock, pay operating costs and add it to its own working capital. If he was unlucky enough to die his securities, dividends and cash might well be kept by his broker instead of being delivered to the proper authorities to be held for the investor's heirs. If, for some reason, an investor wrote to his broker with a com- plaint, he often received no response; if he telephoned, his broker frequently put him off by laughing about what he called a "minor breakdown in routine." Sometimes though, the broker might snarl; at other times he might shame an investor into silence by suggesting that the investor was ignorant of Wall Street's routines. Even at the highest management levels of the Exchange, complaining letters from investors, especially small investors, were referred to as "idiot" mail.

Not that the Exchange itself did not respond. Its Department of Member Firms did process complaints, but it was hardly the kind of policeman most investors needed. Few realized that the Exchange actually and basically is a powerful trade association operated by Wall Street in its own interests. True, the Exchange did put some fifty firms on a number of restricted lists, stopping some from advertising or accepting new business. But in 1968, the year of the back office breakdown—a breakdown that set the stage for failures of many firms in 1969 and 1970—the Exchange felt no great necessity to take real action to cope with the increased volume, even though it knew the firms were still planning massive hirings of salesmen. A survey of fourteen firms by the Exchange in 1968 showed that these alone were planning to train 2,250 new salesmen. By no coincidence it was in that year, too, that the small investor bought some of the most speculative new issues ever offered in the securities markets and bought them at a rate that sent the over-the-counter market, where most new issues are traded, spiraling to unheard-of volume. In fact, trading was so great in untested new issues, most of which are bought by men, that overall stock ownership by men rose above that of women for the first time in many years.

The plight of the individual investor bothered few in Wall Street. Nor was there much fear that the administration would react to the increasing volume of complaints from investors. Flush with money, as they were in 1968, Wall Street's partners had contributed heavily to the Nixon campaign, feeling they were buying protection. Among some of the larger contributions made by Wall Streeters to the Nixon campaign, which cost $10 million to $12 million, were Howard W. Butcher III, a partner in the investment banking house of Butcher & Sherrerd, who gave $55,400 to the Republicans in 1968; Richard J. Buck, a New York broker and chairman of the finance committee of Harsco Corporation, who gave $25,000; Frederick L. Ehrman, chairman of Lehman Brothers, who gave $41,136; Albert H. Gordon, chairman of Kidder, Peabody, who gave $38,750; the late Louis A. Green, a partner of Stryker and Brown, investment bankers, who gave $27,000; David Van Alstyne, Jr., a senior partner of Van Alstyne, Noel & Company, who gave $25,000; Jack J. Dreyfus, Jr., chairman of the Dreyfus Fund, who gave $245,000 to both Republicans and Democrats.

As it turned out, those who felt they were buying protection were right. The doors to the White House itself were open to the Street, with Bernard J. Lasker, chairman of the New York Stock Exchange board of governors until May, 1971, and his successor, Ralph D. DeNunzio (a partner of Kidder, Peabody), frequent and influential White House visitors. In fact, the Street even had a man in the White House, in the person of Peter Flanigan, a Nixon aide who had been a vice-president of Dillon, Read.

Elsewhere in the administration, the SEC fell to bargaining with the Exchange over critical problems instead of making determinations and ordering compliance as it could have under the provisions of securities laws. In 1970, although its own mail and investigations told it of the vast incompetencies and dishonesties in the industry, the SEC blandly allowed the Exchange's member firms to tack a $15 surcharge onto the smaller trades of individual investors, even though the surcharge was not wanted by the efficient members of the industry. Then again, in 1970, the SEC displayed no outrage at all when the Exchange proposed to raise commission rates on small trades as much, at first, as 300 percent (later, it reduced the maximum to 50 percent).

Much the same foot-dragging could be seen in the Department of Justice in those years, though its antitrust lawyers clearly felt the Exchange was violating antitrust laws and regulating the securities industry not in the public interest but in the interest of its *own members.*

Indeed, the only outcry against Wall Street came from Congress, the one institution the New York Stock Exchange feared since the only reforms ever placed on Wall Street had originated there. The Exchange trembled, for example, when Senator Edmund Muskie, the Maine Democrat and presidential aspirant, introduced an insurance bill in 1970 to protect investors from bankrupt Wall Street firms. But if it was fearful, it was not impotent. So great, in fact, was the pressure put on Muskie by the stock exchange that he felt compelled to complain of it publicly. Early in 1971, moreover, New Jersey's Senator

Harrison Williams, a Republican, felt compelled to tell Wall Street, in a series of speeches, that the two years of hearings he was scheduling to investigate the Street's practices were not intended to be "accusatory"—a strange statement for one of the Senate's more able watchdogs, unless one appreciates the power of the Street to discomfort its enemies.

The fact is, as such incidents suggest, that Wall Street has reason to be confident, even arrogant, about its political clout in Washington in recent years. It put the leading Democrat candidate for the presidency in 1972 on the defensive, complaining over rough handling, and forced the chairman of a Senate investigative committee virtually to apologize for what he was about to do—namely, investigate an industry sorely in need of investigation.

The real threat, most of Wall Street felt, was not government but competition as manifested by institutional investors. Impelled by a desire to reduce commission costs, a number of mutual funds, insurance companies, and pension plans had been gnawing away at the Exchange's authority (and its members' income) by undermining the commission rates the exchange fixed and enforced. To avoid the rates—though they did receive discounts for volume trades—the institutions traded exchange-listed stocks elsewhere. They did business at regional exchanges, where the rates were lower, and some even became members of those exchanges. Some institutions began trading through firms, in the so-called third market, which dealt in Exchange-listed stocks for a commission equivalent to a small fraction of the trading price, say an eighth of a point. A number of institutions also traded among themselves, creating what came to be known as the fourth market. Eventually they demanded that the Exchange either adopt a system of negotiated rates (only for them and not for the individual investor) or grant them membership. Either alternative would drastically cut commission payments to brokers, of course. Negotiated rates would be much lower than the rates set by the Exchange, and institutional memberships would simply cut brokers out completely.

While the Exchange was battling the institutions, trying to

maintain its uncompetitive commission rates, only a few men were worrying about the irreparable harm being done to individual investors. Not only were the lambs once again being shorn, but they also were being blamed for the brokers' problems. Most brokers could not handle small trades profitably, and the reasoning was that if individuals had only stayed out of the market, the back offices would not have broken down. Such a rationale involved blatant disdain for the public interest, though concern for it had been one of the prices required by Congress in the 1930s, when it gave Wall Street permission to regulate itself.

As the Exchange's Haack knew, public interest was being badly served. Secret polls had told him just how badly. Now, today, on a Monday in April, 1970, the rest of the senior staff is about to find out, too.

It was on Monday mornings that the weekly meeting of the Exchange's senior staff was held. It was a meeting that bored Haack, who had inherited the tradition from his predecessor, Funston. As used by Funston, the meeting was a time to be filled in on current matters of interest and to determine what needed to be done or undone. However, under Haack, who tended to delegate authority, the meeting became purposeless— except that it gave lower level members of the senior staff some small exposure to Haack, who otherwise kept to himself. But without the interest of the Exchange president behind it, the meeting failed to be a satisfying forum for anyone. As a result, the staff tended to remain silent. To generate interest, Haack had asked Eugene Miller, his vice-president of public relations and advertising, to develop programs for the meeting. Failing to persuade many of the staff to participate, Miller had turned to outside speakers. On this particular Monday the choice had been Louis Harris, the poll taker, who had been commissioned months before by the American Stock Exchange to sound out individual investors on how they felt about the investment environment, Wall Street itself, the SEC, and the role of the big institutions in the market.

A few minutes before the senior staff meeting began, Haack

left his office through the high-ceilinged anteroom where the Exchange's executive secretaries sat. He walked the hundred steps or so along the marble floor of the executive corridor on the sixth floor to Room 602, where the meeting convened. It was a small, red-carpeted room just behind the elegant meeting room of the board of governors. On meeting days when the entire senior staff appeared, only standing room was available for those who arrived last. Such was the situation that day.

As Haack entered the room he saw that most of the staff already were present. Among those who were in close association with Haack was R. John Cunningham, executive vice-president and the man who really ran the Exchange. Bulky, broad, six-feet tall, Cunningham's oval, soft face and surprising alto voice shielded a hard-core executive who prided himself on being a management expert. He came to be thoroughly disliked by some of the Street's partners. He was, however, an ideal Exchange executive; as Haack filled the role of industry spokesman, Cunningham filled the role of industry whip.

Already there, too, was Charles Klem, a large, phlegmatic man who was vice-president of administration. Though not far from retirement, Klem was still an extraordinarily forceful man, able to think on his feet faster than many of the younger men working under him. Seated near Klem was Lee D. Arning, a very tall, pleasant, and verbose executive who tended to laugh a great deal and whose pure white hair was brush-cut. Arning was vice-president of operations and as such held one of the more powerful jobs in the Exchange. Miller, too, was already present. Short, sallow, with a black stubble of beard nearly always evident, Miller had come from McGraw-Hill, Inc., knowing more about publishing than about Wall Street and the laws governing the securities industry. (Miller had once caused a brief suspension of trading in McGraw-Hill stock when, as the company's director of public relations, he was accused of disseminating information to a closed panel of securities analysts, thereby violating the Exchange's and the SEC's "full disclosure" rules and regulations.)

At the front of the room stood Louis Harris with the

American Stock Exchange poll findings in his hand. His organization had developed what was considered a scientific sample of some two hundred individual investors in ten major metropolitan areas. Each of the investors chosen for interviewing was a relatively large and sophisticated stock trader, a person judged to understand the market and to contribute substantially to its liquidity through extensive buying and selling.

Were Wall Street's firms well run, the respondents were asked? Were they honest? Were they giving their customers good service?

The answers to such questions and others were so unflattering that the American Stock Exchange (AMEX) had sat on them for months before deciding to reveal them to the New York Stock Exchange. When the AMEX finally decided to do so, it stipulated that everything Harris disclosed must be kept confidential, discussed only among the New York Exchange senior staff.

As Harris began to speak and enumerate his findings, the counts began to sound like a criminal indictment handed down by a grand jury. Predictably, the senior staff was blandly quiet; most had long since developed a rhinoceros hide against outside criticism. A few took notes, but Haack, as one vice-president noted later, seemed bored by the proceedings, as if he had heard it all before.

The polled investors, Harris began, were nearly unanimous in the belief that Wall Street was giving some institutions preferential treatment. They believed the Exchange was feeding institutions inside information and distributing investment criteria to them before individual investors, whether large or small, received it. A majority of those polled also attacked Wall Street's claims that self-regulation was effective, saying that the Exchange's self-regulation practices were designed primarily to maintain the securities industry's own privileged position rather than to develop regulations that adequately safeguarded all investors. No type of self-regulation, they felt, was adequate for investor protection. Indeed, the industry's only interest, the polled investors complained bitterly, was its own selfish gain.

Only the SEC came in for any praise as most of the polled investors considered it the only agency operating in the securities industry with the individual investor's interest in mind. But even the SEC was inadequate to the task, they felt, and there was a need for government to police the industry more than ever.

The alienation of these two hundred individual investors, Harris said, was extreme:

> The fact that they feel they need more protection points to a potentially very serious situation. If the securities industry's best private customers are convinced that the mechanism the industry sets up to safeguard their protection is inadequate, the element which makes the securities industry successful, confidence, is also in danger. The data revealed about self-regulation should be very disturbing. As this whole report has shown, the experienced private investor who has been a believer in the securities industry is becoming disenchanted. He feels brokers are looking down their noses at his business because it is not as large and important as institutional business. These feelings of alienation are very real. Unless something is done soon to attempt to bring these experienced investors back in, it is not unlikely that self-regulation and the structure of the securities industry will become a thing of the past.

To some of the Exchange staff, the Harris report raised a picture of a Wall Street that had never quite pulled out of the past or shaken off its old self-serving ways. Though in 1970 the financial community may not have been the fleecers of the public it was in the 1920s, and though the average investor was still gullible and greedy—a sucker for a hot new issue because of the perennial urge to get rich quick—the Harris survey bore in on Wall Street malfeasance, if not actual malpractice. It put a cloud over the vaunted self-regulation of the stock exchange, and it clearly raised the question of whether the government was doing its best to protect investors.

Yet to most of the men who heard Harris and especially to Haack, the Street's leading campaigner in defense of the self-regulation privilege, the poll appeared to have little significance. At least nothing much happened—perhaps because on that Monday in April, 1970, there were other problems on Haack's mind. It wasn't just a matter of whether the customers of the Street could be served. There was the very serious matter of whether many investors could be saved from financial ruin. Many Wall Street firms on that very date were close to collapse, victims of their own incompetence. If they did go under, they would take many of their customers with them, for billions of dollars worth of securities belonging to individuals and corporations were held in Street names.

2

Today's problems

At eleven o'clock in the morning on August 4, 1970, amid the half acre or so of plush red carpeting and the forty-foot high gilt walls of the Exchange's board of governors room, Robert W. Haack stood at the president's lectern facing the inquiring countenances of more than one hundred of the Exchange's less powerful people, representatives of its more than five thousand allied members. Though called "members," the allied members are not really so at all but are ranking partners of firms, the principal partners of which hold seats on the Exchange. The meeting was a regularly scheduled quarterly gathering, held in the normal course of events mainly to soothe the feelings of the allied members, who had no formal say about Exchange affairs but were nevertheless obliged to obey its rules and regulations just as if they were voting participants.

It should have been a routine meeting, but Haack's loose-leaf notebook contained references to problems and proposed solutions so critical and agonizing to Wall Street that he felt obliged to counsel that he would not like to see what he was about to say "in the newspapers tomorrow." As it turned out, his request was in vain. In an industry as fragmented as the securities industry information leaks are impossible to plug, and a few of Haack's statements appeared about a week later in the *Wall Street Journal.*

As always, the allied members sat in armchairs arranged in four crescent rows descending in steps from the back of the room to a shallow pit in the front. To the right and front of the members stood an enormous urn of jasper, silver, and malachite, a gift Russia's Czar Nicholas II made to the Exchange when it listed, in 1903, $1,150 million worth of debt securities for trading. To the allied members' left were portraits of past chairmen of the Exchange.

Just one day earlier Haack had given a similar report to the Exchange's voting members, who had not, as far as it could be determined, told anything to the press, though they were regarded as a notorious source of leaks by the Exchange staff. Today, the allied members were hearing the extent of Wall Street's most serious problems for the first time.

The Street had never been in graver peril.

On one side, hundreds of firms were foundering financially under the weight of a bear market that was producing few commissions, was souring the firms' own investments and was spotlighting their inability to remain viable businesses without great floods of money constantly pouring in. On the other side, the growing presence of institutional investors, particularly the mutual funds, to which so many small investors had fled for protection from brokers, was posing a threat to the very existence of the Exchange itself.

Of the two threats, the more immediate was the insolvency of the member firms. Bankrupt firms could take their customers down with them, and unless Wall Street moved to clean its own house, there were men in Washington, aside from those in the Justice Department and the SEC, ready to do it for them in the name of the small investor—among them Senator Edmund Muskie.

The securities laws gave the Exchange the privilege of self-regulation, and the Stock Exchange had decided weeks before that it was time to dispose of the weaklings in its midst. Just a year earlier, Haack pointed out, insolvency had not really been a problem at all, with the exception of a small firm or two, but even then the Exchange was forecasting the end of the "moms and pops," the truly small firms of the industry. In fact, Haack had appointed Lee D. Arning, vice-president of operations, as the enforcer in a drive to merge those on the edge of failure. But the effect had been too little and too late. In mid-1970, Wall Street was skirting massive numbers of bankruptcies among small and large firms alike.

Some firms had already gone under, and Haack had put $55 million of the Exchange's own money, including its new building fund of about $40 million, into the breach, but it was clear that it would not be enough. Already $13.5 million had been used up in the failures of only four firms (McDonnell & Company, $6 million [later to rise to $8 million]; Gregory & Sons, $6 million; Amott, Baker & Company, $1 million; Baerwold & DeBoer, $500,000). "We hope there will be no other firms," Haack said, but he undoubtedly knew that just a week later a relatively large one, Dempsey-Tegeler, would be liquidated at a cost expected to fall between $9 and $15 million, depending on what the Exchange's own liquidator would declare was needed to satisfy customer accounts. Not far from being fingered for extinction, too, were Meyerson & Company of San Francisco; Fusz Schemelze & Company of St. Louis; Blair & Company of New York; Orvis Brothers of New York; and Kleiner, Bell & Company of Beverly Hills.

Haack said nothing, either, about how close to bankruptcy were some of the Street's true giants: Goodbody & Company, Francis I. duPont, and Hayden, Stone. If any one of them went down, hundreds of thousands of customer accounts would go with them, and, in the aftermath, all of Wall Street as it currently existed would follow, for an angry Congress and even a friendly administration would be forced to act.

Even as Haack addressed the allied members, Hayden, Stone was being lent $5 million. Before long it would get another $7.6 million and be forced into a merger with Cogan, Berlind, Weill & Levitt, a small but highly profitable firm with institutional accounts. Within months, Goodbody would be hustled into a merger with Merrill Lynch, a reluctant partner that would demand and get from the Exchange guarantees against losses up to $20 million as part of the deal. DuPont would be teamed up with Glore, Forgan, and in April, 1971, it would be taken over by H. Ross Perot, a Texas millionaire who was eager to acquire duPont but who also insisted that he be protected against losses by the Exchange: he extracted a promise of indemnification up to $15 million.

The Exchange would try to give some firms no help at all, among them First Devonshire Corporation and Charles Plohn & Company, two New York firms with no clout at the Exchange. Instead of being offered cash or merger partners, these two firms were suspended and handed over to the SEC with the statement that they were in "such financial condition that they could not be permitted to continue in business with safety to their creditors or to the Exchange." (To the credit of the SEC, it forced the Exchange to make good the losses of their customers.)

The Exchange's statement with respect to First Devonshire and Charles Plohn was one that could easily have been hung on the doors of one hundred or more Wall Street firms, the financial conditions of which were so shaky that they were in continual violation of both SEC and Exchange rules governing capital. Those rules required the firms to maintain a debt to capital ratio of up to 30 to 1. Most Wall Street firms had gone well beyond that, and, said Haack to the allied members, there was even one firm (which he refused to name) with a ratio of 1,500 to 1. In any case the Exchange, he said, was lowering the ratio to 15 to 1. Furthermore, a ratio of 12 to 1 would be enough to bring on the run a special committee of six men headed by Executive Vice-President R. John Cunningham.

For the most part, the capital and debt structures used to measure Wall Street firms are uncomplicated. Capital originates principally with the general and managing partners, who are required to invest high liquid assets such as cash, bonds, and stocks as the price of joining a firm. A relatively small portion of capital originates with limited partners, who frequently are favored employees invited to share in the firm's profits by investing in it. Another source of capital is the cash and securities of customers with large, or primary, accounts. In the financial structures of the firms, such additions to capital are carried as subordinate loans. If insolvency occurs, the loans are repaid before the capital of the partners is extracted but not before the investments of the firms' other customers.

The debt structure of Wall Street's firms consists of only a few more parts than that of other businesses. There are the usual costs, such as fixtures, rent, taxes, sales commissions, and entertainment. But the firms' debt also includes underwriting commitments as well as bank loans to carry margin accounts and the accounts of cash customers who do not pay their bills in the five days agreed on. To carry cash accounts beyond five days the firms borrow to cover the money due them.

None of these factors created much unmanageable debt, however. The accounts payable that ran up the fastest by far was the entry that resulted from "fails." When Wall Street's back offices began to break down on a broad front in 1968, the failure to deliver stock between firms created debt so great that it is still largely uncounted. And it was this debt that was the chief reason for violations of the capital ratio rules set by the Exchange and the SEC.

Fails were not nearly the whole story, however. Incompetent and greedy as always, a great many firms, in an effort to parlay their capital stakes into immense profits, managed their money in the manner of the crap-shooting investors they supposedly despised. Instead of prudently putting their money into investment grade stocks and, to stay somewhat liquid, into short-term Treasury bills and cash, many firms had bought highly volatile "performance" stocks. In the 1969 and 1970 bear market these were the hardest hit securities, and the capital of firms hold-ing them was diluted accordingly.

Many firms had gone even further in their speculations and had bought letter stock: corporate securities sold privately by very young, unlisted companies that need money but cannot meet legal and other SEC requirements to register a public offering. Letter stock was valued at next to nothing even in the bull market of the late 1960s, but the firms that bought it nevertheless set an arbitrary value on it and included the figures they manufactured in their capital structure totals.

It would have been easy to spot what Wall Street's firms were up to in their maneuverings had their books been open to scrutiny. But their books were closed even to the Exchange and the SEC. The Exchange relied on quarterly financial reports filed by the firms, reports that were faked in many cases. Many partners refused to accept losses of their capital by admitting the insolvency of companies whose stock they had purchased and they did their utmost to cover up such losses. Even after their firms had been marked for investigation, some partners faced down the Exchange's liquidator, a relatively low-level employee, until the Exchange brought in ranking execu-tives from healthy firms to make the confrontations. Five officials of Dempsey-Tegeler went so far as to decide to sue their liquidator.

"The problem of insolvency," Haack said to the allied mem-bers, "was more critical than the world will ever know." The Exchange's job, he said, was to "keep the members in business, not put padlocks on their doors." This, he felt, would be best for everyone. "At one time," Haack said, "thirty percent of the Exchange's member firms could have been put out of business." Just several weeks earlier, in June, 1970, the Exchange's vice-president of public relations and advertising, Eugene Miller, had been saying in private meetings that fifty percent of Wall Street's firms could easily be put out of business.

If the Exchange had not forced mergers as it had and lent money, Haack continued, "Six hundred thousand to seven hundred thousand customer accounts would have been immobilized, and the government would have had to pony up hundreds of millions of dollars. It was a question of whether we could protect the public." Haack, using a lightly veiled species of blackmail, had been calling on influential congressmen all summer, trying to persuade them to stay out of Wall Street's problems since government interference might precipitate the very crisis everyone wanted to avoid. Furthermore, he had implied that if the government did interfere, it would put itself into a position of being partly responsible for investor losses and thus might have to reimburse the firms' customers.

The argument had worked well. There had been little outcry from Congress. Within the administration, the Justice Department was strangely quiet over the mergers forced by the Exchange, although in some minds there were clear violations of antitrust laws. Even the SEC, the agency required through a whole series of laws written in the 1930s to oversee the industry, acted as though it were an arm of the Exchange and initiated few moves of its own. Indeed, some of the senior staff of the Stock Exchange were sure that the threat of so many bankruptcies was exactly what was needed to force the SEC to look sympathetically at a raise in minimum commission rates for which the Exchange was asking.

Whether the Exchange's board of governors really wanted to protect the investing public, as Haack said, was debatable. While the Exchange had committed all of its special trust fund of $55 million to insolvencies, it did so only when it was convinced that if it did not, there was a chance Congress might try to take away its privilege of self-regulation. For years Sam Rosenberry, the Exchange's counsel and a member of the prestigious Wall Street law firm of Milbank, Tweed, Hadley & McCloy, had warned everyone in the Stock Exchange who disseminated information to avoid suggesting to anyone—the press, legislators, and the general public—that the Exchange's special trust fund existed to secure investors against loss. On the contrary, the Exchange's stance was that it had *voluntarily,* even nobly, used the fund to assist customers of some firms— but only firms of the Exchange's choosing.

The Exchange was to give up this position of pretended altruism in the fall of 1970 after a number of suits had been brought against it by customers of firms the Exchange had refused to protect. A number of embarrassing questions about playing favorites were to be put by Representative John E. Moss, a California Democrat and chairman of a House commerce subcommittee that was revising an investor's insurance bill. (The bill, which was introduced in the Senate before going to the House, was important to the Exchange. When passed, it provided $1 billion as a reserve from the U.S. Treasury to supplement a $50 million pool created by industry premiums. In addition, it created a semipublic watchdog corporation— the Securities Investor Protection Corporation—controlled in large measure by the Exchange.)

On August 4, 1970, however, all such developments were in the future. At that time Haack implied clearly enough that despite the troubles born of failing firms and investor protection, there was no reason to believe the Exchange could not extricate itself from them. It was clearly inferred by his listeners, including some of the senior staff, that it was a matter of letting some firms go broke—and the customers be damned. Despite their seriousness, insolvencies did not threaten the existence of the Exchange itself. To be sure, there might result a much smaller industry, but that development was regarded as inevitable.

The growing presence of institutional investors was another matter, however. They not only had bypassed the Exchange again and again in their trading to avoid paying high minimum commissions but had corrupted the Exchange's members, many of whom negotiated big block trades for the institutions in private, then took the trades to the floor of the Exchange for consumation to avoid a charge of violating the Exchange's rule prohibiting off-floor trading.

Though blocks of stock traded in this way nearly always appear on the Exchange ticker tape within fractions of the last price, or even exactly at the last price, thus creating the illusion of being arrived at through the bid and ask routine of the auction market, the truth is that few people really know when price agreements have been reached in secret. Negotiating in secret is of extreme importance for the firms and institutions involved since even a rumor that a big block is overhanging an issue can send its price on the Exchange down—as it should—and can undermine the agreement reached in private.

It is ridiculous to suppose that the Stock Exchange's ticker tape reflect's the workings of an honest auction market when a stock moves an eighth, for example, on a 200-share trade, then moves only another eighth, or not at all, on a 40,000-share trade. The truth is that the firms who take big blocks to the floor for trading are frequently making under-the-counter markets—negotiated trades—in those stocks. Indeed, the firms frequently act as dealers to please their institutional customers and buy stocks from them at prices higher than those the stocks would fetch in bona fide trading on the Stock Exchange floor. The firms then carry the stocks in inventory until they can be sold for a profit. Thus, they become third-market operators, in a sense operating in competition with their own Stock Exchange.

The practices of such firms violate the Exchange's 200-year old condition of membership that grants no breaks or discounts to non-members, that is, the institutions, and outlaws bypassing the Exchange's specialists, whose role of making markets in stocks is, after all, at the heart of the auction market. When "block positioner" firms, as they have come to be called, take a trade to the Exchange floor after a price has been agreed on in private, the bid and ask characteristics of the auction market are ignored. In fact, Wall Street for years has really operated two different markets—the bid and ask market of the Exchange and a negotiated market.

Out of this duplicity there has emerged a situation in which the rich institutional business is monopolized by a minority of well-financed and highly competitive firms—among them Goldman, Sachs; Donaldson, Lufkin & Jenrette; Salomon Brothers & Hutzler; and Merrill Lynch, Pierce, Fenner & Smith. So well entrenched are these and other firms in institutional trading that in the bear market of 1969 and 1970 not one complained of falling profits. On the contrary, profits were up, and at least one firm, Salomon Brothers, hit an all time high.

The monopolization of institutional business has irritated the rest of the Exchange membership—not, of course, because the block firms are parasites in an auction market the liquidity of which is maintained by millions of individual investors; the interests of the smaller investors are of little import to most members. What really disturbs them is the fact that most of them cannot break through the monopoly and reap the profits themselves.

It surprised no one, therefore, that one of the first questions asked of Haack by an allied member, when the president turned to the threat posed by the institutions, was more an accusation than anything else. "Is it not the inability of the Exchange floor to handle large transactions that has fostered the monopoly?" the questioner asked. "Are not these blocks of stock really negotiated off the floor?"

Haack answered, "Some of what you have heard is true, yes; but this is exactly why we're looking to improve the performance of the specialist—his size, his capital."

The response hit at the heart of the Exchange's life or death problem, since it raised doubts about the capability and role of the specialists. To maintain an orderly progression of prices, as they are charged with doing, the specialists match buy and sell orders brought to them by floor brokers. To keep the market liquid, which they are also responsible for doing, they are required to buy for their own account when there are more sellers than buyers and to sell from their own inventories when there are more buyers than sellers.

But most specialists are small businessmen with relatively limited resources. Without much inaccuracy, they have been referred to by some critics as candy store operators. In price breaks of any size and duration, they have time and again been unable to maintain either orderly or liquid markets because of their limited resources. For the same reason they have been unable to take on big block trading, and thus they have *contributed* to the institutions' flight from trading at the Exchange.

Indeed by 1960, when institutional trading began to grow substantially, the market had outgrown the specialists. But they were men highly resistant to change, and because of the number of seats they held and their control of the board of governors, they succeeded in committing the entire Exchange membership and policy to preserving their interests. They have even elected board chairmen from their own numbers.

Thus, when Haack answered the allied member's question by saying, "We're looking to improve" the specialist's size and capital, he was only referring to a plan hatched by the board to persuade the block positioning firms to use their accumulating wealth to back the specialists. The question that no one asked—and the one that still needs to be resolved —is whether the specialist system should be preserved *at all*. On the one hand, it is a far from perfect system, as Chapter 11 shows, but without someone or something—computers, for example—to conduct the auctions in stocks, there would be no market. There would be only a conglomeration of firms dealing with each other on a negotiated basis. There would be little liquidity in such a market and thus no place for individual investors unless they were very wealthy. Though some institutions would undoubtedly prefer to see the Exchange auction market die, the resulting lack of liquidity would raise their costs well above the commissions they have tried to avoid paying for so many years.

Disposing of truly big blocks of stock, 50,000 to 100,000 shares or more, is still handled best on the New York Stock Exchange. Therein lies the essential problem. First, the New

York Stock Exchange is old fashioned, out of date, and dedicated to practices that forestall any attempt at effective solution. Second, any reform presupposes an attack on the heart of the system—the specialists. Third, any solution that involves breaking up the old system must consider the one factor that is essential if a true auction market is to exist—liquidity.

Many solutions have been proposed. For example, it has been claimed that one computer properly programmed, armed with sufficient information, and tied to the offices of brokers and institutions all over the world could replace all the men on the floor of the Stock Exchange—and perform their jobs far more efficiently. This is the proposal that is offered by critics who believe that making a market in stocks is really a job for clerks and point for proof to third-market firms such as Weeden & Company, where clerks do indeed make markets in nearly three hundred Exchange-listed stocks.

Giving the job to a computer is not so farfetched. At least four computerized communications systems now in existence conceivably could evolve into a computerized exchange. One is the Exchange's own Block Automation System (BAS), a communications network sold to brokers and large traders on a subscription basis. Another is AutEx, a system much like the Exchange's but which preceded BAS, while still another is called Instinet. A fourth computer system already in operation is the over-the-counter market's NASDAQ. This electronic system stores the bid and ask prices quoted by a number of market makers in particular stocks. Thus it provides not only a truly competitive auction market but a very real threat to the Exchange specialist system.

3

It was always that way

Iɴ 1967, on the occasion of its one hundred seventy-fifth anniversary, the New York Stock Exchange published a poster reproduction of a painting. The painting, which is lodged in the Smithsonian Institution, depicts a number of thin-lipped, unsmiling men dressed in bright royal blues, reds, and purples, seated and standing at a table placed under a large buttonwood tree growing on Wall Street. To many in Wall Street the scene is comparable in significance to the one depicting the signing of the Declaration of Independence.

It was on May 17, 1792, the story goes, that twenty-four brokers met under a buttonwood and signed an agreement to organize a central marketplace for securities trading. Out of this grew the New York Stock Exchange, which, the tale continues, helped to promote the idea that the average man can share in the nation's growth by buying securities. What the tale does not say is that the average man has always been a loser more often than a winner in Wall Street and that as a small investor he has been regarded chiefly as a source of revenue to float the sophisticated financial maneuvers of Wall Street's imperious insiders.

Well before and long after the meeting under the button-wood tree, Wall Street's approach to finance and investing was a matter of powerful, moneyed, and politically connected interests speculating on the basis of inside information and thus creating financial speculations that the average man seldom could take advantage of. The men involved in the speculations, appropriately preceded on the Street by resident Captain Kidd, were so ruthless that over the years they sheared the public, and they sheared each other. They clearly regarded the individual's pocketbook as something to be picked and the U.S. Treasury as something to be exploited. They used bribery, payoffs, deceit, and treachery routinely, yet they were pious in the extreme and gave generously to charitable organizations. Taken together, such activity became a template of conduct for the manipulators and lawbreakers who have streamed through Wall Street over the past two centuries: including Jacob Little, Daniel Drew, Jim Fisk, Jay Gould, Cornelius Vanderbilt, J. P. Morgan, John D. Rockefeller, and Richard Whitney.

Some of Wall Street's shady practices turned up right at the beginning of its history. Since its residents were political insiders, often leading figures of the day and members of the government itself, the temptation to speculate and then to eliminate risk was enormous. One group of Wall Streeters, for example, arrogant even at that early date, proposed to make George Washington king. The ultimate bribe, it was not the first that Wall Streeters would offer U.S. heads of state in the years ahead. Attempts to influence presidents became routine, in fact, and not all chief executives were as outraged as Washington—or, later, Ulysses S. Grant. Grant, who eventually was ruined financially by Ferdinand Ward, a Wall Street swindler who operated a brokerage in partnership with Grant's son, was requested by Jay Gould not to sell government gold at a time Gould was trying to corner the gold market.

It was natural enough for Wall Street's speculators to get into the habit of hobnobbing with presidents. The government of the United States was first located in Wall Street, and George Washington actually took his oath of office there. Moreover, from the beginning key political figures encouraged the speculators and even helped them. One such politician was Alexander Hamilton, a man determined to reorganize the national debt and to found a federal banking system. For reasons of expediency, he made possible the first great insiders' swindle, thus setting the precedent of "insider" trading—a major problem to this day.

In 1789, after Hamilton had become secretary of the treasury, he issued his Report for Redemption. By year's end, in anticipation that a Hamilton-sponsored bill would be pushed through Congress to redeem at full value the scrip paid to Revolutionary War soldiers, at least three well financed insider syndicates began operating in New York, Philadelphia, and Boston. They bought up soldiers' scrip for pennies on the dollar. One syndicate was headed by Robert Morris, a signer of the Declaration of Independence, a governor-to-be of New York, and a close associate of Hamilton. A member of another syndicate was Connecticut's Jeremiah Wadsworth, a member of Congress who had Hamilton's confidence. Wadsworth sailed to the southern states with two boatloads of agents and money and paid virtually nothing to former soldiers for all the scrip they could obtain.

Hamilton's redemption plan got through Congress but not without help from his opponent Jefferson, who demanded, in return, that Hamilton support him in relocating the capitol to Philadelphia (out of the reach of Wall Streeters) for a period of ten years. The next phase, according to this plan, was to move still farther south to Washington. Besides being indirectly responsible for getting the capitol moved, Hamilton's redemption plan resulted in the first issue of securities traded publicly—a series of government bonds. By 1792, the year the Stock Exchange was formed under the buttonwood tree, trading volume in these bonds was already high.

From the beginning, the Exchange's members were an exclusive group, tending toward monopoly by pledging "ourselves to each other," solemnly promising to charge established commissions to outsiders, and giving each other preference in negotiations. It is true that there was no auction market—there were not enough trades to maintain one—and that stock transactions were negotiated. Yet the private club already had been established, and it was always to operate at the expense of outsiders, especially the small trader. Moreover, the Exchange immediately assumed the prerogative of self-regulation, though in the years ahead it was to act more as a coatholder than as a regulator in matters of members' transgressions against the people and even against the country.

As early as 1834-1835, for example, the Exchange stood by as its members reacted to a land speculation craze by driving railroad and canal shares up 300 percent or more in a few months, aided and abetted by banks, which granted enormous amounts of credit to encourage the speculation. In 1836 land prices fell, giving rise to the panic of 1837. Some Wall Streeters were hurt as share prices plummeted, but, more important, as a result of the Exchange members' greed and the Exchange's lack of control, the entire U.S. economy was staggered. Banks failed everywhere. Worse, some states repudiated their debts, and unemployment soared.

By definition, as its members have scrambled to secure for themselves the greatest profits, the Exchange has failed to carry out its self-appointed self-regulatory function. The Exchange has been riven with dissension, the struggles of factions, and internal warfare. In fact, one of the better known trading techniques, the short sale, was a product of such warfare and was developed as a technique for ruining other men.

A short seller sells shares he does not own. The shares are borrowed by his broker for delivery to the buyer. The short sale is "covered" when the short seller actually buys the same amount of stock he borrowed and returns it to the original lender. His hope is to buy the stock he must replace at a lower price than that for which he sold it. The difference in the two prices is his profit.

The originator of the short sale was Jacob Little, a Wall Street manipulator who, like short sellers who followed him, thrived on dashed hopes and panic. In the panic of 1837, Little, the first professional bear, sold and sold—buying low to cover his sales—and made a fortune as securities values were destroyed.

Little's inspired short selling gained him a great many enemies, and their efforts to destroy him produced the "corner," another Wall Street technique developed primarily to ruin others.

A corner could be made only when the stock issues of a particular company were relatively limited and the wealth of one man or a small group of men was sufficient to buy up, or "corner," the supply of stock. Once, in 1837, when Little was selling short the shares of the Erie Railroad, a group of Exchange members tried to buy up all the Erie shares available so that when the time came for Little to cover his short sales he would have to pay these men, his enemies, whatever they asked. He would have been the first victim of a corner if they had had their way.

The group aligned against Little, which included directors of the Erie Railroad, was, however, at least one jump behind him, for Little resorted to another device—a corporate security called a convertible bond—to get himself out of trouble. Through agents in England, Little bought block after block of the Erie's convertible bonds—bonds that could be exchanged for common stock—and on the day he chose to cover his short sales, he merely converted bonds for stock.

For years such conversions by short sellers, later including Daniel Drew and Jay Gould, gave the convertible bond a shadowy cast. Even today the convertible bond is a suspect security because when converted to common stock, it adds to the floating supply and thus dilutes the stock's value. In recent times corporations have tended to issue convertible preferred stocks as well as convertible bonds—with the same effect. Early in 1971, for example, the outstanding common stock of Occidental Petroleum Corporation totaled 53,056,209 shares. However, Occidental's capitalization also included three separate issues of convertible preferred stock, which upon conversion, would add nearly 16,500,000 shares.

Another technique commonly practiced in the last half of the nineteenth century was "watering" a company's stock, that is, adding to the stock supply without adding to the company's supply of cash or property. Watering stock obviously diluted the value of the original shares, and the device was used by insiders to insure hefty profits. At a time when people bought a corporation's securities on the basis of its assets, not on earnings expectations as they do today, watering the stock of a corporation hurt those who had bought shares in good faith because their equity was diluted without their agreement. In the latter part of the nineteenth century, when watering stock had become routine, Daniel Drew, the originator of the term, gave the device an added dimension.

When Drew, chairman and controlling shareholder of the Erie Railroad, faced a challenge from Cornelius Vanderbilt, who was trying to gain control of the company by making purchases of Erie stock in the open market—that is, through the Exchange—he discovered that the Vanderbilt fortune was being dissipated in the fight. Drew saw his opportunity: he had an additional 100,000 shares of Erie stock certificates printed, and he sold them through Exchange brokers to the unknowing Vanderbilt for $7 million. The sheer scale of the watering of Erie stock was unprecedented.

If slick trading moves such as watering stock reached their peak in the hands of manipulators, greed, cruelty, and dishonesty reached their peak with the consolidators who succeeded them and built huge companies. Among the consolidators were James J. Hill (railroads), John D. Rockefeller (oil), Andrew Carnegie (steel), and J. P. Morgan (banking). Working in concert with Wall Street, which devised a variety of securities issues for their use, the consolidators used every means available, including coercion and violence, to build their empires.

One of the most ruthless consolidators of all time was John D. Rockefeller, a man who surpassed even Jay Gould in reputation for cruelty. Obsessed with the idea of putting together his Standard Oil trust, Rockefeller used whatever tactics served his purpose. For example, he once conspired with the New York Central, the Erie, and the Pennsylvania railroads to give him kickbacks on oil freight charges incurred not only by Standard Oil but by twenty-one competitors as well. Rockefeller's conspiracy with the three railroads enabled him to cripple the twenty-one companies to such an extent that their owners were glad to sell out and to accept the Standard Oil stock he offered them.

Rockefeller's actions, as might be imagined, were one reason why as early as 1880 a political group, the Anti-Monopoly Party, was formed to oppose him and the other consolidators. It took ten years for the group to become effective, but by 1890 the Sherman Anti-Trust Act had been passed. Although the act broke up some monopolies, including Rockefeller's, American business continued to expand, often at a boom rate, and the number of stock issues floated by Wall Street expanded accordingly.

The most serious problem was that many a stock issue was nothing more than a fraud. In the years 1919 to 1933 alone, the public bought no less than $25 billion of worthless stocks with virtually no interference or objection from the Exchange. Much of the time an eager and gullible public bought new issues as fast as they came out. But when there was hesitation, Wall Street nearly always found some gimmick or other to *make* the public buy.

A common ploy of promoters was a promise to pay large dividends immediately, which they did—out of the money they received from the stock sale in the first place. Paying dividends immediately had the desired effect of driving up the price of the stock and insuring greater and greater sales. Then when the price was high enough to satisfy the promoters, the insiders sold out their own shares.

Another technique intended to convince the average investor to buy stock was for a management intent on buying up another company to pay prices for the object company's stock well above its worth. This was especially the case in the great fights for control of railroads. In 1929, for example, the Pennsylvania Railroad bought 223,000 shares and, therefore, control of the tiny Pittsburgh & West Virginia Railroad for $170 a share, or $38 million. The going market price, which had resulted from the railroad's management bidding against J. P. Morgan, was $140, but the stock had been as low as $10.

Such acquisitions suggested growth, and the average investor, eager but well removed from insider circles, usually bought stock in the companies doing the acquiring. With just enough exceptions to encourage him, the average investor bought into a house of cards, responding to a technique so effective it was still being used by conglomerate companies in the 1960s to create the illusion of growth. Companies such as Ling-Temco-Vought, Gulf & Western Industries, Litton Industries, and scores more bought hundreds, even thousands, of small and large companies, paying little attention to earnings prospects. In the bear market of 1969 and 1970, the shares of the conglomerates led the market decline, and early in 1971 their annual reports were full of back-of-the-book notations that detailed massive writeoffs.

In the early 1900s and in the late 1960s getting the small investor to buy often was itself the goal. In the case of the conglomerates, such buying tended to push up the price of the conglomerates' stock, thereby putting it into a better position to borrow greater and greater sums from banks on the basis of its ever more valuable common shares. The borrowings, in turn, were used to make new acquisitions. In the earlier days, however, the motives were much simpler. When the price of the parent company's stock rose high enough, the shares were sold by the original promoters.

Another technique developed to lure buyers was the shadow trading account. This account was maintained by a stock's promoters with a Wall Street broker, and its purpose was to support a high stock price. In a continuous buying campaign, the promoters forced up the stock's price and at the same time created an appearance of interest and activity. Their only costs were brokers' fees since they were buying and selling among themselves.

Devious practices were not confined to fly-by-night promoters, as might be imagined. Some of Wall Street's most prestigious investment bankers—including J. P. Morgan, Kuhn, Loeb, and Dillon, Read—maintained trading accounts of new issues they had brought out. As public buying became more prevalent, the banks disposed of their own inventories of stock, which often had been acquired at low option prices as part of the terms for bringing out the new issues in the first place. For example, half of a $5.4 million profit made by Kuhn, Loeb in creating Pennroad, a holding company formed in 1920 for the Pennsylvania Railroad, was made by exercising options. The options, granted at no cost, gave Kuhn, Loeb the right to buy Pennroad shares at $16 and $17 a share. On the day the investment banking firm exercised its options, the shares were selling for $25.

Even when a corporation operated as a viable business, the average investor was used only as a means of supporting the control of the insiders or helping to finance their frauds. There was the classic case of National City Bank, for example. Under chairman Charles E. Mitchell, a man who dominated it between 1929 and 1933, the bank changed from a century old commercial enterprise with enormous prestige to a firm with an avaricious desire to sell securities. In doing so, National City Bank strayed wildly from the prudent activities of banking, which is largely a matter of accepting deposits and lending money for legitimate business purposes. Instead, the bank sold securities at a rate of $1–2 billion a year. So many of the new issues it sold lacked value that Mitchell once admitted to Congress that they had been "manufactured."

In 1927, for reasons unknown, National City lent $30 million of its own funds to segments of the Cuban sugar industry, in return for which it gained control of some properties in the industry. But the sugar business in Cuba collapsed, and to bail itself out National City turned to its own stockholders. It sold them $50 million of National City Bank stock and gave half of the proceeds to an affiliate, which used the money to buy all the shares of a new company, General Sugar Corporation, a shell organized by the bank. General Sugar spent the $25 million buying up all the bad loans made to the sugar industry by National City Bank. Then National City wrote down its investment in General Sugar to $1. Thus, its stockholders, who had bought the $50 million issue to begin with, salvaged the investment in a deal reminiscent of watered stock. Indeed, it was not until federal hearings revealed it that the bank's stockholders learned where their money had gone.

Stock issues were also used, as they are now, to help insiders retain control. One of the simpler ways involved the issuance of different *classes* of stock. One stock might be called Class A and pay high dividends, but it would have no voting power. A second class of stock, say, Class B, would be issued and retained by management. Though it might pay dividends only after the Class A dividends were paid, or perhaps pay none at all, Class B stock would carry all the voting power and, consequently control. Sometimes the control stock was a Special Preferred, Preference, or Special Preference issue. Sometimes the control stock gave its holders only a minority control, but the effect remained unchanged. Control of a company remained in the hands of the control stock's holders. In the early 1960s, the common shareholdings in General Dynamics of Chicago financier Henry Crown were converted to a Special Preference stock. Crown then proceeded to direct the course of the company, though his original common shareholdings had amounted to less than 15 percent of the outstanding General Dynamics shares.

One of the most effective financial devices ever developed to insure control by a few while the public paid the bills was the holding company. The holding company was a product of Wall Street's most devious minds, and the way it was put to use created some classic examples of fleecing the lambs.

Take, for example, Pennroad, the Pennsylvania Railroad's holding company. It was formed in 1920 by a Wall Street investment banking firm, Kuhn, Loeb, and its leading partner, Otto H. Kahn, to enable the Pennsylvania Railroad to engage in empire building while fighting off O. P. and M. J. Van Sweringen, two J. P. Morgan-backed railroaders who were trying to take over the "Pennsy." Kahn founded Pennroad with an issue of $87 million of voting trust certificates, 97 percent of which were sold to the railroad's 157,000 stockholders. Another issue was sold to the general public, and it raised $45 million more.

The trust certificates, an infamous device in themselves and one seldom used today, gave no voting power to their holders. Instead they specified that voting power lay with three trustees of the Pennsylvania Railroad. The three immediately began using the money thus acquired to buy up railroads in competition with the Van Sweringens and Morgan, who, incidentally, had raised their own funds in the same manner—by forming a holding company and issuing securities.

In the end, the Pennsylvania successfully thwarted the raiders but at enormous cost to the original Pennsylvania Railroad shareholders and to the buyers of the Pennroad certificates. The trustees had paid huge prices for their acquisitions, some of which were worth only fractions of the price put on them. Thus, Pennroad's holdings were carried on its books at far greater value than they were worth, while the ability of these subsidiaries to earn income was questionable at best. In 1929, when panic hit Wall Street, Pennroad certificates, which had been sold initially for over $50 a share and had soared far higher in subsequent trading, fell to $1.50. Eventually, the company disappeared. The Pennsy's shareholders suffered too. From a price that frequently was well over $100 a share, Pennsylvania Railroad Common stock fell to $1.62½.

The most insidious and far reaching example of how the holding company was used to take control is that of Samuel Insull. Through public sales of stock, Insull and his family built a pyramid of 95 holding companies that controlled 255 utilities. Through just one of those holding companies Insull controlled the entire network.

One of the main reasons such companies were able to flourish was the New York Stock Exchange. The Exchange had no rules against listing holding companies that were only pieces of paper bearing an intricate description of a corporate legal maze devised by lawyers and Wall Streeters.

In fact, in creating a market for holding company stocks, the Exchange was certainly party to a promotional scheme, perhaps a conspiracy. Once a company's shares were listed, it acquired the sort of pedigree that helped to create the liquid market it needed if the company was to peddle the shares of additional corporate shells. Theoretically there was no limit on how many holding companies, or shells, could be incorporated. Certainly, the Exchange imposed no limits.

Calls for reform went virtually unheard at the Exchange on the grounds that it was merely a marketplace. If a stock moved up or down sharply, it was a result of supply and demand. If a company wished to list its shares for trading and it met the listing requirements of the Exchange, the shares could be listed for payment of the usual fees: that, no more, no less, was the Exchange's position. And yet, the very fact that the Exchange allowed trading in certain shares implied tacit connivance. Without being able to list them, the securities of many a suspect company might well have become just another obscure over-the-counter stock.

Even today, the Exchange's "passive" stance is far from being impartial. The conglomerates of the 1960s, for example, could not have been nearly so successful in raising money for acquisitions if their initial securites had not been listed on the Exchange. There, they were bound to receive greater attention from the stock-buying public.

In the past the Exchange has blinked at other practices too, including unethical forms of stock manipulation such as the wash sale. Far from condemning such practices, in fact, the Exchange defended them vigorously before a Senate committee that spent seventeen months during 1933 and 1934 investigating Wall Street corruption. The Exchange president, Richard E. Whitney, insisted that the Exchange had exercised a "very real responsibility to the public, as to the securities listed." But no one believed him. The Exchange had done too little in the public interest for too long. The committee, headed by Ferdinand Pecora, who later became a member of the SEC, developed recommendations that formed the basis of the first laws regulating both the securities and the banking industries.

Four laws were eventually passed. One was the Securities Act of 1933—the Truth in Securities Bill—which required the creators of new securities to give the public all the relevant facts before trying to sell them. The bill, as described by President Franklin D. Roosevelt, told "the seller to beware."

Another bill, the Banking Act of 1933, forbade commercial banks from floating securities and being stock market plungers. It also forbade bank officers from being officers of investment banking houses. At the same time, it required private investment bankers to stay either in the deposit-accepting business or in the underwriting business. As a result, the National City Bank, the Chase Bank, and even J. P. Morgan, which had been more of an investment banking firm, chose to stay on the deposit-accepting side of banking.

A third bill, the Public Utility Holding Company Act of 1935, was aimed primarily at the Insull empire. It forced utilities holding companies to register with the SEC to determine whether they served any useful purpose. Voting power was put legally into the hands of the stockholders. The utilities fought against the bill viciously, even to the point of disobedience after its passage and in court cases in which the utilities persuaded judges to hold hearings without summoning witnesses for the other side.

The most potent of the four laws that came out of the Pecora investigations was the Securities Act of 1934 since it created the Securities and Exchange Commission. In doing so, Congress forced the Exchange and its members to answer for the first time to authority outside the confines of Wall Street.

Unfortunately the law did not take away the privilege of self-regulation. In the years following the law's passage, self-regulation was the means by which the Exchange blocked the efforts of the SEC to regulate its affairs. The Exchange, in effect, was able to perpetuate itself as a virtually private club.

Still, the 1934 law put restrictions on Wall Street that had not existed before. It limited brokers' borrowings, which often fueled an overheated stock market, and it outlawed such manipulative securities dealings as wash and matched sales. It gave the Federal Reserve Bank authority to fix margins on stock buying, and it cut the foundations from under the kind of massive short selling that depressed stock prices unnaturally. The law stated specifically that a short sale could be made only after a security had traded at a price higher than the last sale.

The SEC, which was created to enforce the securities laws, remained very much a paper tiger until 1937, when a new chairman, William O. Douglas, the future Supreme Court Justice, insisted that the Exchange reorganize to remove some of the power of the floor traders, including the specialists, who were resisting any sort of change. Before 1937 the Exchange was organized in much the same way as any other club, relying on committees for its administration. Its president was a member whose administrative responsibilities were not so heavy that he could not tend to the affairs of his own firm as well. President Richard Whitney, for example, was running the affairs of his firm on a full-time basis. Douglas proposed that the Exchange be put in the hands of professional managers or a staff. As a result, William McChesney Martin, a young

Exchange member at the time, developed a reorganization plan that met with the approval of the SEC but, as expected, not of the Exchange members.

The plan called for a full-time paid president and a new board of governors (to include brckers who were not members and even members who lived outside of New York). Further, it called for election of governors who represented *the public* and for a major revision of the Exchange's committee system.

The plan, with little chance of being passed by the Exchange's board, languished for nearly a year. Then on March 8, 1938, an extraordinary event occurred in Wall Street. The Exchange suspended its own president for dishonesty—the same Richard Whitney who had testified before the Pecora Committee about the Exchange's "responsibility." Since 1926, as it turned out, Whitney had been stealing the securities of his customers to cover his own bad investments. Within a month, by April, 1938, Whitney had been tried by a court and sentenced to a jail term of five to ten years. Within another month Martin's reorganization plan had been adopted, and Martin himself was made the Exchange's first professional president.

Ever since the implementation of the Martin reorganization, there has been an Exchange staff headed by a paid full-time president. In the years before Keith Funston and Robert Haack, the presidents hired by the board of governors responded completely to the Exchange's own interests. Under Funston and Haack, however, a widening schism developed, first because Funston despised the coarse men of the Exchange floor and threatened to quit many times, and, second, because Haack saw in the Exchange something far more important than a private club. Like Martin thirty-three years before him, Haack called for reforms.

The Exchange has done little to improve its service to the investing public. Likewise, the SEC has generally been remiss in its actions. True, there have been investigations by the SEC, but they they have been *friendly* investigations. The SEC has moved quickly against flagrant lawbreakers but has been content to propose and suggest rather than to order and demand broad change. It has stepped lightly in deference to the Exchange's legal power of self-regulation, and only strong SEC chairmen such as William Cary in the 1960s have been able to introduce changes.

The reforms of the 1930s certainly improved things for investors. But these measures did not make Wall Street honest —just *less dishonest*. What is desperately needed is an end to self-regulation, the removal from control of men whose only interest is their own, and the development of a market that serves everyone. All of Wall Street's history cries for nothing less. All of Wall Street's present condition makes such change mandatory.

Part 2

Inside the firms

4

Wall Street, the Exchange, and the investor

WHEN G. Keith Funston, a Pied Piper, led millions of Americans into the stock market during the 1950s and 1960s, he did so with promises of riches. The Exchange was at a peak of power and influence, and in those days the Exchange's staff—especially Funston—saw its major task as one of educating Americans in ever greater numbers to buy stocks. In the 1950s, few Americans knew how the Street longed for them, and in the Exchange the decision was made to educate them—to put them through a conditioning exercise. It would be a campaign well worth the effort in the Exchange's view. The average American's disposable income was rising rapidly. Yet he was saving less and spending more. In his affluence, he was inclined to buy stocks. Collectively, he was worth millions of easy commission dollars to Wall Street, and he had only one or two shortcomings. First, he was abysmally ignorant of how easy it was to buy stocks, which sometimes deterred him from making purchases (however, when hooked,

he often became an addict). Second, he was also basically
ignorant of Wall Street's ways and jargon, which also deterred
him from plunging.

Thus, the need, as it was seen by the Stock Exchange and
by just about all of Wall Street, was to educate the public,
and with education would come a bonanza of commissions.

The campaign that was initiated with advertising and public
relations staffs (which tripled in number during Funston's
fifteen-year term) was the brainchild of the Exchange. And
as is the case today, the Exchange determined exactly what
the industry would say about itself, both by originating material for its member firms and by censoring and editing whatever copy the firms themselves developed. The editing and
censoring were intended not so much to prevent the firms
from misleading investors as to prevent one firm from disparag-
ing another.

In 1968, for example, the Exchange seriously considered
forcing member firm Edwards & Hanly to discontinue a series
of television advertisements using endorsements by celebrities
(for example, Joe Louis), that implied to some viewers that
the firm was stronger than others. At another time the Exchange itself delayed the distribution of its official publication,
The Exchange, in order to delete the names of the few Wall
Street firms that had reorganized and spent money updating
their back offices. It was decided that to mention their names
would, by omission, sully the names of the rest of the member
firms.

Determining what course the Street would take in com-
municating with potential investors goes back to the 1960
publication and distribution of "The Investors of Tomorrow,"
a self-serving public opinion survey taken by the Exchange.
This document reported that "Americans favor broad share
ownership," that "millions of them were thinking about investing," and that "more of them realized they can invest on a
modest scale." The survey reported further that the "public is
reluctant to contact brokers" and didn't even "know the location of brokers' offices." From these observations, the writers

of "The Investors of Tomorrow" drew a clear conclusion: "Potential investors," they decided, "want basic information about securities."

The survey was the first stroke, to use a Wall Street phrase, in making a market. After the survey results had been distributed, the Exchange's own advertising and the advertising of member firms carried a message suggesting that brokers were friendly, that they could help to increase personal assets, and that their offices were just around the corner. The Exchange itself adopted a motto—"Own your share of American business"—that appeared on every letterhead, booklet, and pamphlet printed by the New York Stock Exchange. (The motto was hastily dropped in 1969, although it continued to appear on proposals made to the SEC.)

In the years following the 1960 survey, the Stock Exchange and Wall Street's brokers flooded the United States and nearly a hundred foreign countries with booklets printed by the millions. Generally, the pieces of literature were distributed free by the Exchange or by member firms, which bought them from the Exchange at a little above cost for handouts to promising customers. Most of the booklets dealt in trivia or, at best, in bland facts, and they carried such titles as "The Public Be Served," "Shareownership, USA," "Investors' Notebook," and "Investors' Primer." They explained the difference, for example, between dividend and ex-dividend, margin and margins, the prime rate and the discount rate, and a stock and a bond.

One booklet still published today, "Understanding the Stock Exchange," is a bland account of the Exchange's internal organization; it offers no explanation of why the various departments exist, only that they do exist. The title of another booklet, "Now, About the Specialist," suggested that at last there was to be an explanation of this activity and the basic conflict of interest involved (a specialist buys for himself yet determines what investors will pay for stocks he controls). Unfortunately, the booklet never deals with this subject.

As the booklets rolled off the presses, the Exchange's re-

search department in the tower of the Exchange building at
11 Wall Street whipped out study after study that showed
how public ownership of stock was growing in terms of numbers, sex, education, age, and a whole variety of other demographic variables. Indeed, few categorizations were avoided,
though the Exchange did not attempt to determine how Jews,
Catholics, Protestants, or other religious groups stacked up
as buyers of securities. Most of the studies amounted to appeals
to the herd instinct, suggesting that buying stocks must be
safe because people were in the market in great numbers.

One of the places where the Exchange's research material
has appeared religiously is in its official magazine, *The Exchange. The Exchange,* in fact, shows true finesse in getting
across the message to the public that *stock buying is good.
The Exchange,* which promotes the idea of stock ownership, is
not a giveaway. It is a paid subscription magazine with a
120,000 to 150,000 circulation that can be audited any time.
One must almost admire the shrewdness of the Stock Exchange
in getting subscribers to its house organ actually to pay for
the pitch delivered by *The Exchange* magazine. At its circulation peak in the 1960s, *The Exchange* was bringing in well
over $450,000 yearly from subscriptions alone. For the most
part, subscribers are average investors living in all fifty states
and more than ninety countries. Many unrealistically view
the Stock Exchange as paternally interested in their welfare.

Magazine publishing, booklet distribution, and demographic
research have been only a part of the Exchange's educational
campaigns, however. The Exchange has produced films, one
of which was shown on television 1,000 times in a single year,
and has persuaded 400,000 or more people a year to view the
Exchange floor from a visitors' gallery. Few people seemed
to mind the bulletproof shield between them and the trading
floor or the ubiquitous squad of armed guards.

The Exchange's own advertising campaign, geared to the
small individual investor, nearly always carried the "Own
a share of American business" phrase along with some hard
sell. But the advertising—more specifically, its placement—

was designed to gain even more space than the Exchange paid for. It was in the 1960s that the Exchange's advertising in seven hundred newspapers was switched from the general news sections to the financial sections. The switch was intended to persuade newspapers to carry stock tables in part or in full as editorial content. At least one newspaper objected: the *New York Post*. The *Post*'s owner, Mrs. Dorothy Schiff, contended that the exchanges ought to pay her to carry the tables since the tables amounted to advertising. However, many a newspaper went far in the other direction. Some wrote long articles on the virtues of shareownership. A few, the *New York Herald Tribune*, for example, actually carried stock analyses written by reporters. Others sponsored investment forums and lectures, using materials, speeches, and even formats provided by the Exchange. In 1964 (a year selected at random), the Exchange acknowledges that over thirty thousand lectures, based on Exchange materials, were delivered in forums sponsored by newspapers, local libraries, and business groups.

Even colleges and schools were not immune. In fact, they became the targets of a special department of the Exchange, which reported directly to the vice-president for public relations and advertising. Again using 1964 and figures developed by the Exchange, its public relations staff participated as lecturers in 40 workshops, conferences, and teacher training courses attended by 2,000 secondary school teachers from 19 states. The staff concentrated on explaining "the fundamentals of investing" and was able to boast that in the year 1963-1964, 25,000 teachers instructing some 2.5 million students were using Exchange teaching aids in classroom studies of the stock market.

A serious questioner might well ask: "Well, why not? If investing is part of everyday life in the United States, shouldn't the fundamentals be taught early?" The answer is yes, of course. But the meaningful issue is not whether people should be taught investment fundamentals at an early age but whether the teaching should be restricted to only what a powerful vested interest group *wants* them to know. Are people truly being taught to be intelligent investors? Or are they the victims of a Wall Street hard sell?

Know your broker, the Stock Exchange's representatives have told many classes of would-be investors throughout the United States. The truth is that knowing your broker is an impossible task for most people. Facts that are truly relevant, particularly negative facts, are rarely given out by the Street to investors—and never voluntarily. It has nearly always taken a law or a scandal to bring such details out into the open.

The opposite is much more likely. Brokers tend to know far more about investors than investors know about brokers. Though they operate in an industry not notable for divulging much about *itself*, brokers require today's individual investor to tell all, giving personal and bank references and even providing a statement of citizenship. Nevertheless, it is a rare customer who, in turn, asks about the financial condition of the firm or the background and qualifications of the salesman facing him, even though he is entitled to know both. It is a rarer broker who volunteers that information, although in the light of Wall Street's 1970 insolvencies the answers to such inquiries are of crucial importance.

How many customers would like to have known, for example, that the firm they were dealing with was itself buying restricted stocks, that is, stocks with no ready market, and assigning them a high arbitrary value as part of their firm's capital. Yet the purchase of such stock by at least one company —McDonnell & Company—contributed to its insolvency. How many firms actually went under because of such purchases can only be guessed at—undoubtedly there were dozens—for such information is kept secret not only by the firms but by the Exchange and even by the SEC. The loser, of course, has been the investing public. Instead, the nondisclosure of such information has led investors into a fool's paradise at a time when proper discretion would, rightly, have warned customers away.

Secrecy is part of Wall Street. The skeletons have been carefully locked away for years. Indeed, many a Wall Street move has been covered up when disclosure of facts would have been an aid to investors. For example, even after many of its members became corporations—and one, Donaldson, Lufkin, Jenrette, had sold stock in itself to the public—the Exchange did nothing about requiring its members, corporations or part- nerships, to tell as much about themselves as it insisted corpo- rations reveal in order to be listed on the Exchange. A few member firms published annual reports voluntarily, but even these carried a minimum of meaningful information. When change did come—in 1970—it was only because the Exchange feared the SEC might force even greater disclosure. Only then did the Exchange's Department of Member Firms advise the board of governors to issue a new minimum standard for dis- closing financial data. Not surprisingly, the Street threw a veil of secrecy around a mushrooming problem of securities theft as well. Though theft had been rising sharply all through the 1960s it was not until May 13, 1969, that the Exchange's De- partment of Member Firms advised the board of governors that securities theft was now a serious problem. The concern was not so much a matter of checking dishonesty. Wall's Street's firms had been content for years to let the stealing go on as long as they had insurance companies to pay for the losses. But now, thefts were mounting so severely among member firms that insurance companies were refusing to write fidelity bonds, even at sharply higher premiums, to cover partners and employees of Wall Street firms.

The problem had become acute by late 1968 and early 1969 after a Nashville firm, J. C. Bradford & Company, had reported to the Exchange a fidelity insurance loss of $1 million. Brad- ford's insurer, Aetna Casualty and Surety Company, canceled the firm's blanket bond, and although it issued a new binder, Aetna spelled out to Bradford how the firm would have to improve screening of new employees and change its ways of operating. Most significantly, Bradford had to agree to an ex- traordinary deductible of 92.7 percent. In other words, if Bradford reported a $100,000 loss, the brokerage firm would be obligated to pay $92,700 back to Aetna after the insurance company had paid the full claim of $100,000.

A similar requirement was forced upon W. E. Hutton & Company, a house based in Wall Street. On May 1, 1969, the United States Fidelity & Guaranty told W. E. Hutton that it would no longer issue surety bonds. U.S. Fidelity already had paid out $700,000 in losses resulting from the disappearance of securities at the firm and was the defendant in a case brought by Hutton concerning other claims. Hutton went to Continental after U.S. Fidelity's refusal but was turned down. Next it went to the Hartford Fire Insurance Company, which did agree to issue a blanket bond but only on the condition that Hutton accept a $50,000 deductible clause applicable to *each* claim.

The reluctance of insurance companies to insure brokers against loss through theft was based on hard fact. Between 1956 and 1959, 57 percent of every dollar in premiums was paid to cover losses. Between 1960 and 1963 the figure was 67 percent. It grew to 79 percent between 1964 and 1967.

On November 24–26, 1969, an industry-sponsored conference on "Security Control" was convened in New York to discuss ways of tightening up the Street's lax security. The conference was a high-level one, for those attending were the Street's highest ranking executives, including the Exchange's vice-president of operations, Lee D. Arning. Also present, because of their obvious expertise, were Thomas Dolan, a New York Police Department sergeant who was head of the Department's Stock and Bond Unit (months later, in 1971, Dolan would exclaim in disgust over the hiring of a known securities thief by a firm because the man was "a good worker"); Dr. Robert R. J. Gallati, director of New York State Identification and Intelligence System; Murray J. Gross, assistant district attorney of New York County (who in June, 1971, would describe theft in Wall Street for Senator John McClellan's investigating subcommittee as a "free for all"); Wallace R. Mosely, director of special investigations for the William J.

Burns International Detective Agency; Robert M. Morgenthau, U.S. Attorney at the time for the Southern District of New York.

In the opening hours of the conference, Wall Street's problem was keynoted by one of its own—Frank G. Zarb, a senior vice-president of Cogan, Berlind, Weill & Levitt, Inc., and chairman of the Joint Bank-Securities Industry Committee on Securities Protection. Said Zarb, a back office executive: "We have failed to secure our industry from criminal elements who have demonstrated an ability to profit handsomely from our weaknesses."

Despite Zarb's warning and despite the expert advice gained at the conference, stealing continued unabated and on a fantastically large scale. More than a year and a half after the conference, for example, a clerk walked out of F. I. duPont Glore Forgan & Company with $1 million worth of IBM stock folded up in a newspaper. Other victims of stealing were the Morgan Guaranty, L. F. Rothschild & Co., Marine Midland Grace Trust Co., First Devonshire Corp., G. H. Walker & Co., Wertheim & Co., McDonnell & Co., Goldman Sachs, Hayden-Stone, and Wood, Walker & Co. Expert estimates of the extent of the stealing varied widely, but had one thing in common. The amounts stated were enormous. On June 8, 1971, Attorney General John N. Mitchell said that by "conservative estimate" more than $500 million worth of securities had been stolen in the past two years—in other words, in a period beginning just a few months before the security control conference. The estimates of Robert Haack were not nearly so large, but clearly showed a rising trend of theft. In June, 1971, he told the McClellan subcommittee that lost and stolen securities totaled $56 million in 1970, $41.1 million in 1969, and $33.6 million in 1968.

Obviously, many investors who did business with those brokers involved would like to have known the extent of the securities thefts, particularly if the salesman suggested the customer leave his excess cash (at no interest) with the broker and his securities in the broker's name for safekeeping and convenience. At the beginning of 1970, that excess cash, which is carried as a "free credit balance" in the brokerage's bookkeeping accounts, totaled $2.5 billion just among members of the New York Stock Exchange.

How safe that cash was depended on the firm. The firms that went under, in the usual Wall Street practice, mingled customers' cash with their own. As for the value of stock certificates left in Street names by both cash and margin customers, indications are that it totals hundreds of billions of dollars. The value of certificates frozen during 1969 and 1970 in the accounts of defunct brokers is not known, though it is known the Exchange's $55 million Special Trust Fund fell far short of being able to make good all the losses. Moreover, the salvaging of Francis I. duPont required $20 million from H. Ross Perot, a Texas manufacturer, while the assets of Merrill Lynch were needed to salvage Goodbody & Company.

For those investors who had listened to Funston and the Exchange and then lost cash and stock or found that they could get hold of neither, the lessons were bitter ones. They learned, if they paid cash, that though they paid well in advance, their stock certificates sometimes took months to arrive. Meanwhile, institutions paid for their stocks only on delivery of the certificates. Many customers with margin accounts also learned the real meaning of a pair of previously unknown words that appeared on the standard margin agreement they signed: hypothecation and rehypothecation. To margin customers they can mean, and have meant, a complete loss of their investment.

When someone buys securities on margin, as the phrase goes, he puts up only a percentage of the cost and borrows the rest from his broker. In recent years, the cash requirement, determined by the Federal Reserve Board, has varied between 70 and 90 percent. The broker keeps the purchased securities as collateral even though he may well have lent the investor as little as 10 percent of their value on the day they were bought. This is hypothecation.

The cash resources of most brokers are limited to the capital supplied by their partners or to their profits in investments;

even in bull markets few brokers retain enough cash to be able to lend much. They therefore take customers' securities and pledge them at the banks that grant "brokers' loans." This practice is called rehypothecation.

Rehypothecation is legal, and it has been tested in the courts. It may even seem fair to some investors. Most investors are unaware, however, that a lending bank's claim to the securities is *superior* to both the broker's and the investor's, and that the bank can sell the securities without telling anyone. Thus, if a broker should fail—and many have—his margin customers can easily end up with losses far beyond the amount they were lent by the broker to buy the securities originally. Their investment, which may have been as high as 90 percent of a stock's value, can be totally lost. In fact, only a court order in the fall of 1970 prevented the Morgan Guaranty from selling rehypothecated securities it had accepted from First Devonshire, a brokerage firm that went under in September, 1970.

Securities customers are also left vastly ignorant in the matter of commissions. When the Stock Exchange began campaigning for higher rates in the spring of 1970, it unashamedly and repeatedly offered the argument that by raising the commission rates charged the small investor by as much as 50 percent the customer would be far better off since brokers would then be able to give him service. Such statements were utter nonsense. By that time, the majority of brokers did not seek business from small investors. Indeed, because he had promised various federal officials that "everyone would be served," Haack had to call for volunteers from among the member firms who were willing to accept business from small investors. Finally, late in the summer of 1970, the Exchange's public relations staff was told that a list of firms who "wanted" small accounts, some of whom were fairly reluctant volunteers, had been prepared and should be given the widest possible publicity. Not so surprisingly, the resulting mail frequently related how the letter writers had been turned away by brokers on the Exchange's list.

Yet, in July, 1971, during a third attempt in two years to

raise minimum commission rates, Haack once again told the
SEC at hearings in Washington that the higher rates would
persuade brokers to do business with small investors. Happily,
the statement was greeted with deep skepticism by Sheldon
Rappaport, associate director of the SEC's trading and markets
division, who suggested that higher rates might well drive away
small investors.

Given the cavalier way in which they have been handled, it
is not too difficult to conceive of the deep dissatisfaction that
exists among small investors. Yet there is good reason to think
today that many have become gun shy of Wall Street's brokers
and thereby less gullible than mere lambs. There is a growing
militancy among them, too, suggested by the suits being
brought against brokers and exchanges. They have demanded
that Congress reform the Street, and they have asked that the
SEC be given greater power. Being fleeced is painful, and
though generation after generation has proved itself gullible
and greedy even after being taken, it may be that this generation of investors will bring about meaningful reforms.

5

Wall Street's partners

B_{ACK} in January, 1967, when Hayden, Stone seemed a fast moving, slick kind of Wall Street company, its top officers gathered one Sunday in the very comfortable Connecticut home of Alfred J. Coyle, Hayden, Stone's chairman and the Wall Streeter who had directed the company's affairs since the early 1960s.

A chief executive who appeared flinty at first meeting, Coyle tended to make his subordinates feel that they ought to stand at attention and his peers adopt a defensive tone. In addition to Coyle, there were present at the meeting Ara A. Cambere, the company's amiable, joke-telling president, and George A. Murray, senior vice-president for marketing. Absent was Donald R. Stroben, Hayden, Stone's crown prince by reason of his work in investment banking, specifically the careful hatching of a series of corporate underwritings for Teledyne, a con-

59

glomerate company whose securities had been one of Wall Street's hottest speculations a year or two earlier.

The reason for the meeting was to discuss image building, or, more precisely, Hayden, Stone's first annual report, which was why there were also men present who represented Albert, Frank, Guenther, and Law, an advertising and public relations firm with a hammerlock on the accounts of many Wall Street firms. Conspicuously absent was Hayden, Stone's own director of advertising and public relations, a bright, intelligent man named Lang Littlehale, who unfortunately had not impressed Hayden, Stone's top management.

Coyle himself was particularly indebted to Albert, Frank, which had developed a series of highly effective ads illustrated with comic drawings of animals—a turtle, for example, to suggest that investors were too slow to trade their accounts. The ads had persuaded thousands of people to open accounts with Hayden, Stone, but Coyle wanted to take another tack.

Hayden, Stone had started out in the nineteenth century as an investment banking firm, but it was not until the 1960s that it attained a reputation as an industry leader. In 1967, however, it fancied itself a pace setter in investment banking, becoming so sensitive to its place among the élite of Wall Street that whenever the company was invited by an issuing underwriter to participate in an offering, Hayden, Stone watched with more than the usual jealousy the place it was assigned on the marquis of firm names in the advertisements. Placement was a way of confirming, as other firms did, its self-assigned status. When the firm name appeared farther down in the ad than expected, the anguish was very real and very great.

On this particular Sunday, Hayden, Stone was finishing its first year as a corporation, having made the leap away from Wall Street's traditional business structure, the partnership. Now, though its shares were privately and closely held, it was obligated for the first time to tell something about itself publicly. As it turned out, the company failed that first test of disclosure abysmally. There was no talk of acting in any interest but that of Hayden, Stone. The company's affairs were nobody's business but its own, and the investor was a mark to be aimed at.

From the beginning of that Sunday meeting, Coyle and the others decided that mere numbers and facts would not do. They were not "creative" enough. "We are concerned," Coyle said in leading the discussion, "about getting into just a re-portorial kind of thing. When you have the creative group of Albert, Frank become involved," he said, with a meaningful look at the two representatives of the agency who were present, "you don't want a straight annual report. You ought to talk about emphasis, theme, and philosophy. We want some kind of message, not just that we have eighty-two offices, and so forth.

"The quality and scope of our investment judgment," continued Coyle, ever the Wall Street salesman, "should be the theme of our first annual report." Then he ticked off the firm's accomplishments as he saw them.

"Underwriting clients for the last five years have had an aggregate sales growth of 300 percent. We do business with a hundred thousand retail accounts, and the rapid growth of these customers indicates we are making money with such in-dividuals, which, after all, is the name of the game. Our computer program stock selection techniques have shown re-markable performance. It is examples of this type I think we can use to emphasize our expertise. If someone can dream up an original format . . ." Again he nodded toward the Albert, Frank men. "Format is vital. That's a starting point. Empha-size service to retail customers," he said. "Emphasize that we make money. Emphasize that we are investment bankers to growth companies."

It was a pleasant meeting for the participants—almost an outing—and they joked confidently about the future. Only occasionally were Hayden, Stone's back office operations men-tioned and then never in a way to suggest that those offices were overflowing with stock certificates and other bits of paper required to transfer stock ownership—in other words, to carry out the stock transaction contracted for by the Hayden, Stone boardroom salesmen when they accepted orders from customers.

For the string of creative writers eventually assigned to write the Hayden, Stone annual report, putting the firm's activities on paper proved to be a task beyond their imaginations. Despite the existence of autocratic rule from the top, the company was discovered to be composed of a series of fiefdoms with separate sovereignties that could be upset only by falling sales. Each key man, whether he was in charge of block trades, municipal bond sales, corporate finance, or over-the-counter dealing, insisted that the firm's health was determined by his activity alone. It was not just pride in accomplishment that the writers ran into but individual arrogance and a disregard for working as a team.

Even in January, 1967, Hayden, Stone seemed out of control. For example, even as its operations were backing up under a flood of orders, Hayden, Stone was continuing to hire salesmen by the score. It finally reduced its academic requirements, lowering them for salesmen from a Master of Business Administration (preferably from Harvard) to a level never spelled out by the head of the training school to the writers who interviewed him. The firm hired the butcher, the banker, and just about anyone who could write an order in legible English.

It also became increasingly noticeable that the company's array of modern computers (IBM's 360 system and others) were programmed for taking orders and were linked to a national network of Hayden, Stone sales offices. The machines also were used to digest data and "pick" stocks. But apparently no one thought of developing computer programming to *process* the stock transaction itself—which was, after all, the reason the customers were paying commissions. As it turned out, the annual report discussed on that Sunday in January, 1967 finally became two publications. As writer after financial writer flunked the Coyle test for creativity and time grew short, the company put out an annual report of the kind Coyle had hoped to avoid—one with "mere" numbers and facts. Late in

1968, however, it was followed by a sales-oriented booklet much like the one Coyle had had in mind. It is ironic, in view of the fact that Hayden, Stone's days were numbered and Coyle himself would soon be ousted, that the booklet's final words were: "We are proud of our past, but the best is yet to come."

In 1969, well before the beginning of the bear market, the roof fell in at Hayden, Stone. The causes were clear-cut: the company was accepting far more orders than its back offices could handle; and it was failing to deliver stocks to other firms and to its customers. It soon found itself well up on restricted lists maintained by the Stock Exchange. It was forbidden to advertise, solicit new business, take orders below a particular value, or accept sell orders from any customers who had not purchased stocks through the company. Hayden, Stone's record-keeping was a shambles, and further sales, the Exchange reasoned, would only aggravate its back office crisis.

The company had also failed to maintain capital in the required ratio to its debt. Though it had borrowed new money to bolster its capital standing, the borrowings were not enough, and Hayden, Stone's future looked bleak, indeed. In the end, to keep the house from going under and taking more than one hundred thousand customer accounts with it, the Exchange persuaded the firm of Cogan, Berlind, Weill & Levitt to acquire Hayden, Stone—in the process giving up $20 million of Exchange money to CBWL as part of the deal.

Hayden, Stone was one of two classic cases in which mismanagement was the cause of the loss of control. The other was McDonnell & Company, a firm that specialized in rights offerings—short-term options granted by corporations to stockholders to buy shares at a predetermined price. During their short life span of two or three weeks, rights are also traded on the exchanges and in the over-the-counter market. McDonnell had also built up a substantial commission brokerage business with the public, so substantial in fact that it was far more than the firm could handle.

The beginning of the end of McDonnell & Company really

began at the Tryall Country Club on Montego Bay, Jamaica, early in April, 1968. From forty-five to fifty of McDonnell's management personnel, including its regional branch managers, had gathered to hear a progress report on the installation of an IBM 360 computer and electronic data processing system that was, everyone said, to cure McDonnell's back office ills. Present to head the discussion were members of the firm's family of owners: T. Murray McDonnell, Morgan McDonnell, and Sean McDonnell.

Like so many other firms, McDonnell & Company had spent large sums to increase its public commission business. It had renovated its boardrooms and put $400,000 into fixtures and a lease on a plush salesroom in New York's Park Avenue. But also in the pattern of other firms, it had spent little on its back office. The policies of McDonnell, as seen by one of its executives, had been to "build dollar volume. The back office would just have to catch up." Thus McDonnell had relied on a relatively slow NCR data card system tied to a pair of NCR computers to process its rising stock transaction volume. The NCR system clearly was inadequate, though, and in the summer of 1967 McDonnell hired a computer consulting firm named Data Architects to devise and install a new set up.

At the Jamaica meeting the following April, Data Architects promised that the IBM 360 system it was installing would be operating by July, 1968. As the consulting firm's plans were disclosed, most of the McDonnell executives felt reassured. One or two, however, began to feel uneasy. Data Architects had never done any computer programming before for Wall Street, and handling stock transactions is a unique process. One man asked how Data Architects "can design software for the computer if you have had no experience with stock transactions or knowledge of the back office." The answer he got did not reassure him, and later he said, "They seemed to know nothing about the business."

Still, Data Architects insisted that by July 1, 1968, a few months hence, the initial phase of the system—the "customer trade cycle"—would go on stream. Further, the entire system—

Street side accounting in which brokers deal among themselves, included—would become operational in three phases extending over a period of twelve to eighteen months.

One branch manager questioned whether the new system should be implemented without retaining a back up. He suggested keeping the NCR system working in tandem until the IBM was fully operational. The McDonnell back office on lower Broadway near Wall Street was too small, he was told, to accommodate both the NCR computers and the new IBM machines. In fact, one of the NCR machines had *already* been taken out. It was risking the survival of the firm, the manager responded, to effect the IBM replacement without maintaining a backup. He was prophetic. Even as the conference progressed, the remaining NCR computer caught fire, leaving McDonnell with no processing capability at all and forcing it to farm out its back office work for several days to Shields & Company, a firm with an NCR data processing system, and another firm in far-off Minneapolis.

Hobbled as it was, McDonnell limped along with one eye on its July startup date. But then came delays in programming the new IBM equipment, and McDonnell's clerical employees failed to get the information and instruction they needed. Complicating things further was McDonnell's acquisition of the firm of Ristine & Company, of Philadelphia. A firm with five or six branches, the customers of which generally made relatively small trades, Ristine provided McDonnell with access to the Philadelphia market. But it brought with it an old-fashioned pen and ink bookkeeping system that McDonnell never fully assimilated into its malfunctioning computerized programs. In the midst of the crisis, many back office personnel never imagined that disaster was nearly upon them. The sales goals of the firm were unattainably high, they said, and thus no excess of paperwork could develop. The crisis was already there. By September, 1968, the new IBM system still had not been started up, and a monumental backup of paper developed. The sales force, operating in the bull market of that year, sent sales soaring to new highs.

Finally, after repeated delays, the new system was plugged in during November, 1968—and stopped three days later. "It just didn't work," is the way a former vice-president of McDonnell describes the breakdown. "It aborted. Trades got lost. There were no confirmations. It was as simple as that. It was no wonder, though. What we had was our old NCR system operating at an inadequate rate on top of a new system with hardware that wasn't functioning. As a result, when heavy trading volume aborted the computer programming, there were fantastic breaks in our stock record account, which controls the inventory of stock certificates. This is a basic record. Once it goes, you have a real problem. It affects dividend accounts and the receipt and delivery of securities. At McDonnell the whole back office was out of control. At least one-third of the McDonnell statements to customers had at least one error in them that was impossible to correct. There was no way to do it. If that first phase customer trade cycle had been permitted to run even two more days, McDonnell would have been forced to cease all public business."

As its back office limped along through the end of 1968 and into 1969, McDonnell's failure to deliver stock certificates to other firms mounted until its "aged fails to deliver," those deliveries thirty days or more old, created debt on its books so great that the firm was in violation of the Stock Exchange's rule requiring the maintenance of a maximum 20 to 1 ratio of debt to capital. All the while it also was losing money at an increasing rate as a result of paying large fees to Data Architects, now 25 percent owned by McDonnell.

In the last months of 1968 and in January, 1969, McDonnell did three things. First it kept quiet about an audit taken on October 31, 1968, by the accounting firm of Lybrand, Ross Bros. & Montgomery that showed substantial unreconcilable differences in securities ownership and dividend accounts, differences that clearly placed McDonnell in violation of the Exchange's capital–debt ratio rule—*the Exchange itself said nothing.* Second, to raise money, McDonnell sold unregistered stock to its employees even though public sales of unregistered stocks violated the Securities Acts of 1933 and 1934. This time, is was *the SEC that said nothing.* "The facts told these people," says a former McDonnell executive, "were not consistent with the Lybrand, Ross report either." Finally, McDonnell raided its segregated securities box, taking securities owned outright by customers and forging the signatures of the owners or their trustees on stock transfer powers. *In effect, it stole the securities.*

Early in 1969, McDonnell's principal owners persuaded Lawrence F. O'Brien, the Democratic party's national committeeman and the one time postmaster general, to join the firm as chairman. Undoubtedly unaware of all the facts when he accepted the chairman's position, O'Brien left in July of that year after the firm had issued a press release (believed true by O'Brien at the time) announcing that $3 to $10 million in new capital had been raised. In fact, this was not the case. At an all-day Sunday meeting held in New York's Summit Hotel, O'Brien learned that no hard cash was available. The amounts quoted were merely contingent pledges made by McDonnell family members and by subordinated lenders. On Monday morning O'Brien resigned.

Indeed, it is a puzzle why O'Brien stayed as long as he did or why he joined up at all. All the time he was there, the first six months of 1969, McDonnell's back office costs were completely out of control, and the firm's operating losses mounted at a frightening rate. The problems were plain for anyone to see—especially someone on the inside.

In January, 1969, when O'Brien became chairman of McDonnell, Data Architect's proposed system still was not working. Its fees were enormous, and friction had developed between its employees and McDonnell's in-house data processing people. Each blamed the other for breakdowns as the cost of processing a stock transaction rose to $75, then $85. Even a major attempt by McDonnell to get the system under control did little to right the problem, though it did confirm the diagnosis.

In mid-1969, McDonnell persuaded a back office executive,

Henry Lindh, to leave Faulkner, Dawkins & Sullivan to become McDonnell's vice-president of operations. Lindh only
confirmed what everyone either knew or suspected: the Data
Architect system was not workable. More importantly, even if
it could be made to work, its costs in relation to McDonnell's
volume were excessive. Lindh determined that the system was
geared to handle two to three times the trading volume Mc-
Donnell was processing. Based on existing volume, the unit
cost to process a single stock trade was estimated at between
$40 and $45. Cost accounting studies showed that McDonnell
could afford only $6 to $10—$15 at most—to process each
stock trade.

In September, 1969, Lindh abandoned Data Architect's program, and six weeks later he brought in the Automatic Data
Processing Service Bureau in a last attempt to reduce and control costs. He still hoped to save the firm. But straightening
out McDonnell's back office proved to be an impossible task.
Errors had been compounded and run into both the old and
the new systems. There was no way to undo what had been
done. "We were putting garbage into the system, all the old
errors," said an executive. "We were getting garbage out."

By late 1969, the outlook was clearly grim for McDonnell.
Indeed, it looked so bad that in March, 1970, the Stock Exchange stirred itself and began liquidating McDonnell—at a
cost to the Exchange's Special Trust Fund of $8 million. A
month later, in April, the SEC revoked the firm's registration
and license to operate. At the same time, McDonnell's management consented to SEC findings that it had failed to exercise the kind of supervision that would have prevented
violations of the Securities Acts of 1933 and 1934.

Unfortunately for investors, McDonnell and Hayden, Stone
are *typical* New York Stock Exchange firms, as typical as is the
Exchange's failure to regulate until too late. The inability and
disinclination of Wall Street's partners and corporate managements to *manage* is widespread and not confined to medium-
large companies, such as Hayden, Stone, or to relatively small
firms, such as McDonnell & Company. Basic incompetence has

touched some of the very largest houses, including Francis I. duPont, and some of the smallest, including J. W. Sparks.

In the case of duPont, its management practices contributed to a profitless stalemate that forced it to merge with another firm, Glore, Forgan & Company, and both, in turn, absorbed Hirsch & Company, an old-line member firm with a good base in international business. Even the merger and acquisition proved to be inadequate to keep duPont above water, however, and new capital was acquired from Texas industrialist H. Ross Perot, who consequently gained control. Before duPont merged with Glore, Forgan, the Stock Exchange levied some of the stiffest fines ever recorded on duPont's leading partners for failing to administer properly the complaints of customers.

Like many of Wall Street's firms, duPont's back office had broken down in 1968 and 1969, but the firm ignored hundreds and probably thousands of complaints from customers who were the victims of the breakdown. For this, the Stock Exchange fined the firm $50,000. It also fined duPont's chairman, Edmund duPont, and its managing partner, Charles Moran, Jr., $25,000 each. Moran, who had been sole managing partner for twenty years, was forced out, though not until September, 1969. The firm's third largest stockholder and a man who had swung considerable weight in the firm, Morris Goldstein, also left, though not until after the duPont merger with Glore, Forgan.

DuPont's problems stemmed from back office chaos and from the maintenance of unprofitable sales offices. In 1966, for example, it operated a network of ninety offices in the United States. Only ten of these were profitable, and only another twenty were able to break even. When the stock market boom peaked in 1968, all but one or two of the ninety offices became profitable. But with the downturn in stock buying in 1969, duPont found itself faced with fixed costs (on a much larger scale) for ninety offices, which had over 500,000 accounts to service. One New York Park Avenue office alone was losing $50,000 a month—$600,000 a year. Another fifty offices were losing money at rates nearly as high.

High administrative overhead was one of the reasons that duPont boardrooms piled up big losses. But the lack of a marketing program was also a contributing factor. To be sure, duPont had coaxed America for years to "build a second income," but internally its salesmen resented the firm's policy of never providing them with an adequate research department to back up their sales efforts. Indeed, duPont's lack of research staff was one of its major weaknesses. It paid low wages to research personnel; consequently, turnover was great. It also blundered seriously in failing to develop a significant research capability for institutional clients, the most lucrative segment of the securities industry. Salesmen also regarded duPont as weak in obtaining mutual fund programs for them to sell.

These inadequacies tended to lower salesmen's incomes. Consequently, disgruntled as they were, duPont salesmen were likely to accept just about any kind of order for securities, even those they knew would do little but block back office pipelines. They would, for example, accept an order without blinking for 10 shares at a limit, say, of $25 a share. This was the kind of order that duPont processed at a loss of $15 or more. To the alienated salesmen, who still received their third of the commission, it made little difference.

Untold numbers of duPont investors also suffered, for duPont salesmen were tempted to churn customers' accounts, that is, to effect more trades than necessary in order to produce commissions. (This practice, in turn, added to the turmoil in the duPont back office.) In one sense, the penalty duPont paid for its management's mistakes was not great. DuPont was not dissolved, in contrast to McDonnell and others. To be sure it was forced to merge and there were scrambles for new capital and some top executives were jettisoned, but the firm at least survived.

One firm that did not survive was J. W. Sparks Company, a small firm that originally catered to specialists before expanding its retail commission business in the 1960s. The tale of Sparks's passing is undoubtedly one of Wall Street's more depressing stories since it shows how an inept management and lack of planning can ruin what was once a well run, prosperous firm.

J. W. Sparks was founded in 1900 in Philadelphia. From the beginning it was neatly profitable, as its founder, J. W. Sparks, steered it into the business of clearing stock trades for specialists. Sparks the man and Sparks the firm were both highly regarded in the securities industry, and in the decades that followed its founding, the firm weathered the financial panic of 1907, the Great Depression, and other economic disasters by concentrating on servicing ten or so specialist firms that remained loyal to Sparks by choice. The specialists who were its customers made markets and traded in some of the most active blue chips of all—issues such as American Telephone & Telegraph and Brooklyn Union Gas. Eventually, Sparks was clearing nearly 10 percent of all the trading on the Stock Exchange.

Shortly after World War II, J. W. Sparks was joined in the firm by a distant relative, Harold Longwell. A Quaker, Longwell became the controlling partner and ran the firm in an honest and ethical way. Under him the J. W. Sparks Company continued to prosper for Longwell deftly took the firm into the retail commission business. He also developed a protégé, Fred Winterberg, Sr., who kept the back office running smoothly.

Profits in the retail commission business may not have been as large as those made clearing for the specialists, but they were large enough for Longwell to decide in the 1960s to expand again. At first Sparks looked into underwriting and dealing in stocks, but it discarded both as being too speculative, even though profits in both fields could be unusually large. The choice, instead, was to enlarge its retail commission business by establishing branches.

The decision was made in consideration of the firm's ability to operate a back office efficiently—which is what stock clearing amounts to. At any rate, Sparks hired new salesmen, and it opened new offices. It even acquired an office from the rapidly fading McDonnell & Company.

In 1967 and 1968 Longwell was looking forward to retirement. In fact, he had withdrawn much of his capital, become a limited partner, and prepared for the future. Over the years he had been joined in the firm by a number of able men, among whom were Archie Austin, a general partner in the Philadelphia office, and Charles K. Wynn, Sr., a partner who had moved to the New York office in the late 1960s.

In 1968 Austin and Longwell determined to bring in John Weyble to build up the firm's retail commission business. Weyble was an investment adviser who numbered among his accounts Warren H. Phillips, the astute vice-president and editorial director of the *Wall Street Journal*. Weyble had also given investment advice to trustees of accounts in the care of President Nixon's law firm, Mudge, Rose, Guthrie & Alexander. Weyble was a socially active man, belonging to an exclusive country club in New Jersey. He, in short, represented stark change for the conservative Sparks staff, some of whom resented his natty appearance—expensive suits, bright ties, and black and white shoes. Yet, despite the hackles he raised among some of the people at Sparks, Weyble generated selling enthusiasm among the salesmen, and as one customer's man phrased it later, "He was to go full steam on commission business, and I guess we all got carried away."

J. W. Sparks rapidly developed an extraordinary amount of retail commission business, especially in 1968, and the firm's income shot skyward. When the year ended Sparks could count some $5 million in income, a large sum for a firm that size. About half of the income was generated by its retail commission business and half by clearing for specialists.

Unfortunately, industry costs were rocketing upward, too— in fact, for Sparks they were getting out of control. To attract salesmen, Sparks had decided to pay a commission of 50 percent (compared with the 33 percent paid by most other brokerages and the 25 percent paid at Merrill Lynch). The firm also let go its old auditors and brought in Lybrand, Ross Bros. & Montgomery, a well known and venerable company but one that charged far more than did its predecessor. Still, the Sparks partners rationalized, higher initial costs were the price of expansion. And they plunged ahead, confident that the losses in their commission business would be offset by the high profits of the specialist operation.

Sadly, that did not happen. During 1968 and 1969 the retail commission business grew to the point that the back office lost control, and dissension arose among the partners over how to solve the problem. At one point Winterberg brought in his son as a general partner to wrestle with the back office chaos, persuading Longwell to post the $100,000 capital the firm required from a general partner. Yet loss of control in the back office worsened and Sparks began to fall apart.

Back office employees began arriving late in the morning for work and leaving early in the afternoon. No timecards were kept. Two men, supposedly experts in back office computer routines, were hired to help solve Sparks's problem but instead went on long martini-filled lunches and worked late into the night at double-time rates. After they left for better paying jobs in the summer of 1968, nearly two months of the firm's records, including confirmation orders to buy and sell stocks and other material critical in processing transactions, were found destroyed. Sparks was unable to prove that the two men were responsible, and it faced the almost impossible task of reconstructing two months of trading records. It never succeeded, though it tried for a year and a half.

Some former members of Sparks say that the destruction of its records was the coup de grace. A factor just as important, however, was the 1969 decision of the New York Stock Exchange that Sparks had to reduce its business, *including* the very profitable and traditional clearing business with specialists. The end was clearly in sight.

The firm's debt-to-capital ratio had run afoul of both Exchange and SEC regulations, and even infusions of new capital failed to help. Longwell, now at odds with Winterberg, eventually put more capital into the firm, and a salesman persuaded a customer with $1 million in blue chip stocks to turn the account over to Sparks for use as collateral on a subordinated capital loan. (The price for landing the account included a job for the customer's son-in-law, who apparently didn't know the extent of trouble at Sparks, and a finder's fee for the salesman, who did know the extent of the trouble.)

The end of Sparks as a functioning, viable Wall Street firm came on March 26, 1970, with a notice from the secretary of the Stock Exchange, John M. Mulcahy, addressed to Exchange members, their firms, and Wall Street's banks. "J. W. Sparks & Company," the notice said, "has been liquidating its business for the past few weeks. Charles K. Wynn, who is the sole Exchange member of J. W. Sparks & Company, is scheduled to transfer his membership on April 9, 1970. Upon the transfer of such membership, J. W. Sparks & Company will cease to be a member firm of the Exchange and a clearing member of Stock Clearing Corporation."

That paragraph was the epitaph of a firm that had prospered and grown for most of its seventy years. As it ceased to exist, so did the personal fortunes of a number of its partners. Some, in fact, were forced to take jobs as salesmen at other firms—just in time to start selling stocks in the biggest bear market since the 1930s.

A lack of professional management practices among Wall Street firms is nothing new, of course. In an industry where the partner with the most money in the firm makes most of the decisions, the decisions are usually based on how they will affect his personal fortune. Expenditures in back office equipment and programs are hardly popular. Further, in an industry in which the members are sales-oriented—they beam when they are described as entrepreneurs by a press that often envies and admires them—not much time is given over to such a sweaty chore as management planning. This is why so many firms were vulnerable to the one-two punch of the late 1960s. And since many partners had siphoned money out of their firms in good times while building up huge overhead costs (many of them fixed), they were exposed in the extreme when the bear market began in 1969.

It is not that Wall Street's partners have not been told that planning is critical. On November 10, 1969, in the board of governors room of the Stock Exchange, Robert Haack told the industry just how critical the need for planning was. There were 190 managing partners at that meeting, the first of a series of long-range planning meetings for the firms, and Haack warned them that "planning with imagination will be the key to success for the securities industry in the next decade. Coping with the bewildering pace of change will require the most sophisticated and effective management."

Haack's warning was reinforced by another from Irving Pollack, an SEC director who followed Haack at the speaker's rostrum. The industry's problems would not have occurred if the firms had adopted long-range planning as a means of finding their way, Pollack told the assembled managing partners. Despite such warnings and despite the example of the Exchange itself—it formally adopted both short- and long-range management planning techniques—many a Wall Street firm still operates by the feel in the seats of its partners' pants.

It may well be that modern management planning is beyond the understanding and intellectual capacity of many Wall Streeters. Even where there have been attempts to plan, there has been much fumbling. At Goodbody & Company, for example, a sustained try was made in 1969 to reorganize the back office cage. Goodbody's plan was to eliminate most of the paper handling in the stock processing routines, developed in the nineteenth century, and replace much of it with electronic gadgetry. It was a plan that should have worked, but Goodbody put the new system in on top of the old one. Today Goodbody has gone the way of many other inept firms and has become the acquisition of Merrill Lynch.

Even where companies have been able to plan, control is sometimes elusive. Merrill Lynch, for example, maintains some of the tightest controls on Wall Street. It sends partners out to spot check branches by looking into accounts that seem churned and into discretionary accounts (those in which the customer has given the broker permission to trade without consulting him). Yet even Merrill Lynch was sullied a few years ago when one of its vice-presidents and a voting stockholder, Archangelo Catapano, learned through a Merrill Lynch underwriting of Douglas Aircraft securities that Douglas's earnings were about to drop. Catapano, who had been informed of the earnings drop by Dean Woodman, the Merrill Lynch underwriter, relayed the information to mutual fund salesman Lee Idleman. Idleman in turn tipped off a number of funds, including the Madison Fund. All the while Merrill Lynch was advising individual investors to buy Douglas stock. When the conflict was disclosed publicly, Merrill Lynch pleaded ignorance: it was too large an organization to know what everyone was doing. Yet Catapano remained with Merrill Lynch, suggesting at least that the individual investor is regarded as fair game even in the offices of its self-appointed champion.

A pertinent question to consider about Wall Street is whether its managers have learned anything from the débacle of recent years. The evidence and their attitudes suggest that they have not. For example, although managements in other industries today see the computer as an important tool that provides instant data concerning marketing, purchasing, finance, production, and inventory control, Wall Street still views the computer as a stock-picking toy. At best, most brokerage firms use the expensive machinery to get out a payroll or check a customer's credit. Though the Exchange has said that the industry will replace paper work with electronic impulses, most Wall Street partners haven't the foggiest understanding of electronic data processing and how it can be applied to management planning.

There's a lot of learning to do, but it may well be that most Wall Streeter's will be unable to change and that it will fall to younger men coming on to adopt modern techniques and enlightened ethics.

In *New Breed on Wall Street*, Martin Mayer suggests that the "new breed" has already arrived. Mayer holds up forty or fifty men and firms that he regards as examples of the new breed. But to anyone familiar with Wall Street, Mayer's examples do not represent a new breed at all. Not surprisingly, his book was lauded in 1970 by the Stock Exchange, which was desperately trying to build a new image for its member firms' partners. Unfortunately, with few exceptions the men praised in Mayer's book have learned only how to build a better mousetrap. They are managers of other people's money and investments, traders in the market, and men who have moved a little faster than the rest of Wall Street to corner the lucrative institutional business provided by mutual funds, pension trusts, banks, and profit sharing plans.

In fact, Mayer's men are simply Wall Street's next generation of entrepreneurs, exhibiting the same characteristics that made their forebears vulnerable. One Mayer candidate, the firm of Kleiner, Bell & Company, was one of the first in 1970 to be liquidated by the Stock Exchange. Another, Investors Overseas Services (IOS), has been forced to operate only outside the United States. Mayer's new breed, like those before them, are merely Wall Streeters who see obtainable riches and are willing to expend extraordinary energies to get their share. Like those before them, they maintain no formal marketing programs, they talk of research as simply something to sell, and they care little for back office efficiency. The concept of establishing lasting and responsible investment institutions in the best interests of the public is furthest from their minds. Their attitude is clearly spelled out in the advice nearly all of Mayer's men give to the average investor: stay out of the market and buy shares in some kind of investment plan. This is Wall Street's new breed.

6

The analysts

In 1963, after studying the practices of Wall Street's securities analysts, the SEC concluded that Wall Street research, far from being a guide to investing, was merely a selling tool.

In words kinder than they should have been, the SEC said, in effect, that the analysts were Wall Street's whores and their broker-bosses, the Street's pimps. The analysts were under constant pressure from the firms who employed them to write "buy" recommendations for the customer's men. The SEC concluded, in fact, that too often the recommendations were casual ones, written to entice the gullible.

Not much has changed since 1963. Most of Wall Street's research, with the exception of that provided for the institutional investor, resembles nothing so much as tip sheets written by touts. The Street's market letters and research reports are still produced with the "total lack of established standards of research criteria" noted by the SEC in 1963. Few analysts bother —or indeed are allowed by their firms—to check independently the glib estimates of earnings given them by corporate managements anxious to push up the prices of their securities. Most analysts concentrate on the positive side of a corporation's business without mentioning the negatives. Indeed, late in December, 1970, when the bear market seemed to be ending, many analysts were forecasting a boom, while corporate managers themselves were positive that profits in 1971 would not be any better than they had been in 1970. Nevertheless, the touting was clearly effective. The stock market shot up, but the economy itself only struggled along.

At best, analysts are poor investigators of fact. Many fear talking to executives, much less putting pertinent questions to them; executives often seem to the analysts just as formidable as their Wall Street bosses. At meetings between analysts and corporate executives the hard questions are seldom asked, and managements are rarely grilled as they might be by a skeptical newspaper or magazine reporter. The questions posed are so routine and predictable that the public relations staffs of corporations are able to arm their executives with answers weeks before the questions are asked.

For example, not long after Champion Papers merged with U.S. Plywood, in February, 1967, the public relations department of the merged companies initiated a series of seven meetings with various organizations of securities analysts in different cities of the United States. The company regarded the meetings as a series of steps in a major campaign to boost the price of U.S. Plywood–Champion Paper stock, and thus the men scheduled to speak were its highest brass—including Karl Bendetsen, chairman, and Gene Brewer, president. The content of the speeches, however, clearly was not very important; the speeches themselves were given to an outside free-lance writer to prepare, with instructions to cull his material from booklets and pamphlets published months before by the company.

Strangely, analysts jealously bar the press from their meetings. The New York Society of Security Analysts, has a strict rule against admitting reporters, although it relaxes the rule if the corporate guests make a special request to admit a favored or sympathetic newsman. Most reporters and editors of any experience have known for years, of course, that very little news turns up at analysts' meetings, so they are content to stay away. Those who do attend are often on the payroll of a Wall Street firm's house organ or of the corporation for which executives are scheduled to appear. Those that stay away know full well that analysts' meetings, like planned and managed press conferences, are scheduled at the request of a corporation, usually to dispense bullish information that executives wish to plant. Such information is usually old, occasionally trivial, and often irrelevant nonsense. In one speech delivered by Bendetsen, for example, he envisioned the paper-making companies of the United States working on a three-shift basis, cutting trees at night, in well-lighted woods. Bendetsen could also see those companies using every part of the tree, and he drew a comparison with the hog-killing industry, which uses "everything but the squeal." On such information analysts wrote "buy."

The publicity campaigns of corporations should not be underestimated, though. Actually, they are, in fact, highly effective. Nor are they not always mere exercises in sales promotion. Once, Island Creek Coal Company was anxious to get the news out that it had developed large new markets in Japan for its metallurgical quality coal—an expensive, profitable variety. At the same time, Island Creek was about to be acquired by Cleveland– Cliffs Iron Company. For months the company courted analysts and other representatives of Wall Street, greeting whoever turned up at headquarters in Cleveland with open arms. A man sent from *Investornews,* a booklet published until 1970 by F. I. duPont and given away to its investor customers, was received by Island Creek's entire corporate management— seven men in all. The result was a long, favorable profile of Island Creek. Weeks before the duPont man's visit, the Island Creek management had talked to analysts of Hayden, Stone, which had responded by publishing a massive study of the entire coal industry including a very favorable estimate of Island Creek's earnings.

In the weeks following the visit by the duPont man, the Island Creek management also met with the New York Society of Security Analysts, where grand speeches were again made on old themes. Afterward, the stock of the company soared as analysts jumped on the bandwagon. Island Creek moved from the low twenties to over $50 a share. Indeed, Island Creek management had maneuvered the analysts so well and made such bulls of them that Cleveland–Cliffs backed away from acquiring the company because the price of acquisition went too high. Later, Occidental Petroleum bought Island Creek.

Of course, stockholders of Island Creek were not hurt, but not because Wall Street's analysts had developed pertinent investment information. The fact is that most analysts develop little first-hand information. They get their leads, in the main, from stories appearing in the press. Very few analysts are permitted to go into the field (the duPont and the Hayden, Stone men were exceptions), and even then they are limited generally to subway rides between Wall Street and midtown Manhattan where the corporate headquarters of about 150 companies are stationed.

When analysts do get out, they often settle for a meeting with a member of a company's corporate relations staff, a financial flunky assigned to develop optimistic facts and figures by omitting any negative implications. Mobil Oil keeps a man lying in wait on its corporate public relations staff for just such visits. Worse, because financial public relations employees are legally bound to be accurate, analysts often end up in the clutches of someone from a lower management echelon. Often these men are in no position to say what is happening, where a company plans to go, how it plans to get there, what the costs will be, or what the potential profits are. Such subjects are beyond middle management's knowledge or, if not, at least beyond their authority to discuss. An assistant treasurer of

Magnavox, for example, once told a duPont representative earnings were about to rise; actually they were about to fall sharply.

Because of their inability to collect meaningful information, many analysts also become the easy victims of high-powered financial public relations firms whose corporate clients pay them to drive up stock prices by getting analysts to write recommendations. Among such firms are Steve Booke & Company, a New York outfit with eighty corporate accounts including Wells Rich Greene, an advertising agency, and International Utilities, a conglomerate that has grown by issuing a variety of securities called second preferred stocks.

Another financial public relations firm is Hill & Knowlton, which admits publicly that its purpose is to inflate the market prices of its clients' stock issues. Among its accounts are Twentieth Century-Fox, Control Data, Allis Chalmers, Procter & Gamble, American Airlines, and Equity Associates.

Corporate executives hire firms such as Booke & Company and Hill & Knowlton for a number of reasons. One reason is that higher stock prices can make millionaires of the corporate executives doing the hiring since they nearly always hold options entitling them to buy thousands of shares of their company's stock at predetermined low prices. When Wells Rich Greene sold 409,900 shares to the public in October, 1968, Mary Wells Lawrence, its biggest stockholder and chief executive officer, received $1,226,575, for selling only 75,250 shares (at $16.30 per share) of the 301,000 she owned. Her average cost had been 10¢ a share, or $7,525, meaning that she had been enriched by $1,219,050. Richard L. Rich, another principal of the firm, sold 75,000 of his 300,000 shares, which had cost him an average of 17.5¢ each, or $13,125, for $1,225,000. His profit was $1,211,875. Prior to issuing its stock to the public (at a gross price of $17.50 after allowing $1.20 to the underwriter), Wells Rich Greene had been a thoroughly publicized firm.

Inflating the image of a company and consequently inflating its stock price also makes it easier and less expensive for merger-minded corporations to acquire companies they have their eye on. If a corporation pays for an acquisition with stock that has appreciated greatly as a result of public relations efforts, it needs to give up fewer shares. If it pays cash, it can more easily borrow from banks if its stock is strong and rising in price. Indeed, this last method was the one used by conglomerates in the late 1960s. After borrowing, the conglomerate would issue a new security, a convertible bond or, as International Utilities often did, a preferred. Then the proceeds would be used to repay the loan.

The fact is that the pressure tactics corporations have used in recent years to inflate their stock prices have been scandalous, but in Wall Street few brokers have done much to counter them. Few care to annoy corporate managements, especially if an underwriting relationship exists. Often such a relationship does exist since as many as a hundred Wall Street firms can be involved in distributing the shares of a single underwriting— distribution that is paid for by the corporation issuing the securities.

In 1970, for example, hundreds of brokers and dealers participated in a massive distribution of AT&T securities—over $1.5 billion of thirty-year debentures, the buyers of which received warrants to purchase 31,386,540 shares of common stock at $52. The issue was very clearly aimed at the small investor since AT&T made the offering to its own shareholders. In Wall Street Ma Bell received high praise from analysts even though they knew that (1) AT&T's rate structure was under attack by the federal government and (2) Comsat, the communications satellite company, loomed ominously as a true competitive threat for the first time in AT&T history. In 1970, the highest price paid for AT&T stock was $53.87, up from a low of $40.37. Yet, after the debentures were sold, AT&T common languished at $47 and $48 a share—during the bull market of late 1970 and early 1971—and fell as low as $43 later.

In the case of the AT&T offering not one broker developed and distributed an in-depth study that included AT&T's problems though such a study was clearly warranted. At the Stock Exchange, in fact, an established rule against listing and trading rights and warrants was lifted, and a major campaign of hoopla was initiated. In the end, nearly the entire issue was sold, supposedly to the gullible widows and orphans whom Wall Street mythology claims are the owners of AT&T stock. The analysts never seriously considered making any waves; they reacted not at all.

It doesn't take a massive AT&T issue, however, to attract scores of Wall Street firms. Even relatively small underwritings are eagerly sought by brokers, who willingly become beholden to corporations. In May, 1971, a distribution of only 563,400 shares of Reading & Bates Offshore Drilling Company involved fifty-one brokers and dealers. The relatively small offering of Cox Cable Communications—713,217 shares—also in May, 1971, involved fifty-four brokers and dealers.

Many Wall Street firms themselves take positions in stocks, and thus even if analysts employed by such firms feel morally that they ought to report a change for the worse, they seldom do so. The analyst who did respond to an urge to inform his firm's customers of bad news might well find himself looking for another job since securities cannot be sold profitably when a company's outlook is grim. Only a very few firms inform their customers of their holdings, although some larger ones such as Merrill Lynch and duPont have made it a practice.

The silence of stock analysts is not a surprising reaction among men and women who go on day after day developing the same bland facts and then, out of thin air, recommend a "buy" or, at worst, a "hold," and very seldom a "sell." The sameness of their reports, in fact, is startling. Much of the time analysts' research, recommendations, and earnings estimates represent nothing more than the reworked market letters of *other analysts* or the standard fact sheet sold by subscription by Standard & Poor's, a research organization that gathers its material from such sources as newspaper stories, annual reports, and news releases.

The similarity of analysts' reports—it is more accurate to say that they "feed" on each other—is most evident when numbers are discussed. In an issue of *Earnings Forecaster,* a publication of Standard & Poor's, the numbers quoted from different sources sometimes are so close that even the most naive investor would have to be suspicious. For example, in March, 1970, a random date, the estimated 1970 earnings per share of Broadway-Hale Stores were: Standard & Poor's, $2.40; United Business Service, $2.40; Shearson, Hammill & Company, $2.40; Sutro & Company, $2.35. To be sure, there are times when differences show up, but those differences are rarely great. Goodyear Tire & Rubber earnings were estimated in the same edition as follows: Standard & Poor's, $2.50; Shearson, Hammill & Company, $2.50; E. F. Hutton & Company, $2.50; Harris, Upham & Company, $2.45; Goodbody & Company, $2.45; Blair & Company, $2.50.

When there are no new products for an analyst to tout or mergers to exploit, either of which can drive up a stock's price, the analyst may state that a company is "undervalued" in relation to its potential earnings per share. The analyst may also say that a stock's price-earnings ratio—market price of shares divided by earnings per share—is too low. Frequently this judgment will merely be the analyst's own off-the-cuff opinion. If he suggests a higher price–earnings ratio, the number he uses may well be simply pulled out of the air. He may also write, in the jargon so familiar to investors, that "market conditions" or "economic factors" or an "expansionary monetary policy" validates a higher price–earnings multiple.

Though there have been thousands of instances, one classic use of this routine occurred on February 22, 1971, when a Harris, Upham analyst, Francis V. Lloyd III, said of Tenneco, Inc.: "We believe it is reasonable to anticipate a price–earnings multiple of about 15 in a favorable stock market atmosphere." At the time, Tenneco was selling at $27, exactly 11.8 times Lloyd's own estimate of earnings for 1971—$2.30. On May 18, three months after an enormous surge in prices, Tenneco was selling for $26.75.

All too often the result is the opposite. The analysts' touting works, especially if a number of them pile on bandwagon style. A few years ago when Charles Percy left the presidency of Bell

& Howell for the United States Senate, he was replaced by Peter G. Peterson. From a profit standpoint Bell & Howell was in poor condition when Percy departed with much of its manufacturing plant in Chicago standing idle. Bell & Howell cameras just were not selling. Peterson's plan for recovery was to bring in just about any kind of business Bell & Howell could handle. He agreed to a subcontract to make plastic lenses for Japan's Canon cameras; he took another subcontract from Polaroid to make the Swinger camera; and he put the company into making teaching machines. It was a pedestrian kind of comeback for a company with a reputation of glamour in Wall Street, but Peterson took an extraordinary amount of time to court both the analysts and the press. A man sent to his Chicago headquarters sat in his office for four hours, eating lunch with Peterson at the executive's desk. A *Wall Street Journal* reporter received similar treatment. In the end, as favorable profiles emerged, Bell & Howell stock rose in price from the low twenties to the upper forties. Though earnings crept up only slowly, the price–earnings ratio climbed to more than 20 times earnings.

For most investors, earnings per share and price–earnings ratios were magic numbers, especially during the bull markets of the 1960s when they were commonly used to measure a company's performance. For a while it seemed that the higher the price–earnings ratio, the higher the potential of the company, especially among the conglomerates—those companies that resembled holding companies in makeup and the corporate components of which were widely diversified in products and activities. Characteristically, the conglomerate empires were assembled with little regard for earnings. Only "growth," a magic word to accompany the numbers, was considered. Thus, in the bull market of 1968, conglomerate price–earnings ratios soared. Teledyne sold as high as 65 times its earnings; Litton Industries went as high as 56 times earnings. In June, 1970, at the bottom of the bear market, Teledyne was selling for 9 times earnings and Litton, for 8 times earnings!

Only a few people in those bull market days looked to the

traditional measure of a company's worth: its book value; investors who looked for growth used book value only to measure a company's past. The price–earnings ratio was the measure of its future. The higher the ratio, the higher the expected performance, and some glamour stocks even outraced the conglomerates. In 1968, IBM sold at a price–earnings ratio as high as 49, while Polaroid and Xerox sold respectively at 72 and 65 times their earnings.

Analysts never tire of beating the drum for such stocks as well as for newcomers that in some small way suggest they might be the successors of the IBMs and Polaroids. Never, except possibly to favored clients, do analysts clearly say "sell" when the future of a budding company turns sour. Most their new stock issues with the SEC months before the shares analysts merely turn their backs on such stocks and remain silent. The best the average investor can expect is a "hold" opinion, a worthless piece of advice since it is merely the analyst's hedge. "Hold" is proposed hundreds of thousands of times by analysts, and examples of it are found every day. "Hold" was the advice of a Goodbody & Company analyst one day in November, 1970, when Cowles Communications, the publishing and broadcasting company, was planning a selloff to the *New York Times* of its newspapers and a magazine for $50.7 million worth of *Times* stock, "I'd hold the stock [Cowles] if I owned it," said the Goodbody analyst, "though I wouldn't buy it." Any investor might reasonably ask in response to the analyst's advice: "Why, if a stock is worth keeping, is it not worth buying? Why, if a stock is not worth buying, is it worth holding?"

Analysts have also done immeasurable harm to investors by avoiding examinations of new issues that go on the market, especially since the purchase of new issues frequently represents not much more than a chance to roll the dice in a game that favors the corporate issuer and its brokers. Most corporations issuing shares for the first time are shaky little affairs the entrepreneur owners of which head for the public purse as soon as they can get there. To be sure, they must register are sold to the public, and the prospectus that investors are entitled to see is supposed to tell all. The SEC even requires the shakier companies to distribute their prospectus with a thick red line printed on the side of the cover page. In Wall Street, appropriately enough, this species of prospectus is known as a "red herring." But the new issue prospectus—like all others—is written by lawyers expert in developing language designed to dull the senses. It is printed in a format that would discourage all but the most determined reader.

The truth is that the prospectus approach, which is intended as an instrument of required "full disclosure," has been a failure, admitted even by the SEC. New issues benefit the underwriters and insiders, whose options on as much as 25 percent of an issue enable them to turn huge profits overnight. In the 1968 and 1969 bull market many companies took advantage of the compulsive buying that had developed and "went public" only for the quick trading profits that could be made by insiders, underwriters, and the underwriters' favored customers and employees.

Much of the stock that was offered in those years was of equivalent value to wallpaper, as shown in a study by David Clurman, Special Assistant Attorney General of New York. Clurman and a team of investigators studied 103 companies that had brought new issues to market in 1968 and 1969 and discovered a long list of ills. Among the 103 companies, book value was diluted an average of 65 percent and in one case 89 percent. At least 16 companies had never reported any earnings, and another 29 had reported only negligible earnings. One company even admitted in its prospectus that 60 percent of the money it raised by issuing stock would be used to pay past due accounts, loans, back wages, and past due rents. Yet its stock, offered originally at $2 a share, rose to $7.50 before collapsing.

In all this, these companies were aided by Wall Street's underwriters and the brokers who touted the stock. Indeed, Clurman found that many a company was created by an underwriter purely for quick stock profits. In 67 percent of the cases studied by Clurman, the underwriters obtained warrants at a price usually of 1¢ each. The warrants gave the underwriters access to 5 to 25 percent of the stock issue for a three- to five-year period at a price within 10 percent of the original offering price. As in the days when trading accounts were maintained to keep new issue prices rising, the underwriters and their brokers did all they could to stimulate volume and interest. They kept shares out of the market to keep supplies of stock short; they bought heavily for discretionary accounts (for which they could trade without consulting the buyer); and they circulated tips and rumors.

How profitable were those new issues for their insiders? The Clurman study, which unfortunately for investors, reveals no names, recorded the price movements of forty companies after they had brought new issues to market. By January, 1969, all forty had risen in price 50 to 1,000 percent! However, seven months after they had appeared, a sampling of 37 of the 103 turned up the fact that nearly all of them had declined, and that the declines averaged 40 percent of the original offering price. For the small investor, the person who inevitably ended up holding those stocks, the losses had to be substantial.

It has mattered little to analysts or to Wall Street's research firms and their partners that millions of small investors have lost hundreds of millions of dollars due to nothing less than sheer dishonesty. Merely by emphasizing the realities—that new issues indicate untried, often shaky companies—analysts could cool speculation to a great extent. There are few people who read a prospectus. The Clurman study established that most new-issues buyers acted on "hot tips." Yet if analysts had publicized the fact that one company, at least, was trying to pay off its debts with money raised from the public, that new issue might well have failed to sell. Realistically, of course, the analysts who did try to do this would have difficulty getting their views published—in Wall Street, at least. But unfortunately, there is no reason to believe they ever really tried. Back in the days when Peterson succeeded Percy at Bell & Howell, the man from duPont who interviewed Peterson for so many hours attempted to suggest in his report that Bell & Howell was in for some difficult days. The words he wrote were expunged from his copy.

Even after investors get into a stock—whether a new or old issue—they are rarely advised to protect themselves against large losses. In contrast, most commodities brokers talk earnestly and long with their customers about minimizing losses, either through close contact with the broker or by using stop-loss orders. Only a fool would venture into the commodities market without arranging some sort of downside price protection. For many traders the stop-loss technique works well. To use it, a trader merely determines ahead of time at what price level he will sell if a break occurs and instructs his broker accordingly. His purpose is to preserve profits or to stop his losses, as the term stop-loss suggests.

Theoretically stop-loss orders work just as well in the stock markets, but some thinly capitalized specialists on the floors of the exchanges see them as a threat and abort them. In a market correction, stop-loss orders automatically add to the sell orders that specialists have to absorb. Therefore, before a slide occurs —or even if there is merely fear that one will occur—some specialists will reduce a stock's price to wipe out stop orders in their order books and return the price to its earlier (higher) level. A look at the records of the stock exchanges shows any number of such instances. The SEC has dredged them up many times, but one documented instance involving Erie Railroad shares which were traded in the American Stock Exchange, shows what can happen.

After trading had ended one day, the book of the specialist in Erie stock was balanced precisely in a so-called pair-off. The book contained orders to buy 1,100 shares at the market and orders to sell 1,100 shares at the market. Erie closed at 95⁄8. Yet on the next day, the opening trade of 1,200 shares was made at 83⁄4, down 7⁄8 of a point from its closing price of the day before. An investigation initiated as a result of a broker's complaint revealed that the specialist had been carrying a stop order in his book to sell 1,200 shares at 83⁄4 and a limit order (in which the customer sets the price) to sell a similarly large block. Fearing he might have to absorb both orders at the same time if selling in Erie developed, the specialist executed the stop order and bought the shares for his own account. The trade proved to be the lowest in price for the day. In fact, Erie stock closed above the previous day's high of 9⅝. Far from being accused of dishonesty, which was obvious, the American Stock Exchange wrote off the complaint, saying the specialist had exercised his judgment, bad though it was.

Despite opposition from specialists, however, the stop-loss order *can work*. It can be especially valuable in new issues trading and for investors who do not contact their brokers frequently. Yet, analysts and brokers rarely, if ever, suggest their use. On the contrary, they usually suggest that price "support areas" exist (though never for new issues since these are intrinsically volatile) and thereby plant the idea that a stock will not drop below a particular price range. In bear markets, assertions that support areas exist may well have cost investors sums measured in the billions of dollars.

Some analysts defend their upbeat stances by saying that selling touched off by millions of stop orders or even by straightforward advice to sell could generate a market break. Even the New York Stock Exchange has used this reason for banning stop orders in volatile issues, though the real reason more likely was the inability or disinclination of the floor specialists to absorb selling. Regardless of the reason, bans against stop-loss selling deny investors the right to protect their investments and suggest that the system itself is at fault, not the urge of investors to protect their investments.

Some analysts defend themselves by saying that their job is to analyze a corporation's capabilities, its potential for profits, its management, and its markets and then to gauge its chances in the industry in light of the strength of competition and the condition of the economy. It is an argument of utter nonsense, for analysts ignore almost completely the role of the men making markets and determining prices in stocks on the floors of the exchanges and in the over-the-counter market. The fact is that the market price of a stock does not reflect a company's value as determined by the yardsticks applied by analysts. The market price reflects *what people will pay for a stock* and to a large extent the capital and even the personal feelings of the specialist. How else can the action of IBM be explained, for example, when it dropped nearly a hundred points in a year and, based on the 114,000,000 shares outstanding, lost $11.5 billion in value.

Like any other group of people making their living in Wall Street, analysts are urged on by considerations of personal income and their real "job," as they see it, of protecting their *own* interests.

Most analysts, in fact, can be sorted out into three groups. There are those who write research reports and send them simultaneously to all their institutional and individual customers. Such analysts are generally among the lowest in income of the three groups since they depend completely on their employers. Many of these are figuratively chained to their desks and turn out routine reports on industries they are assigned to follow. Often their reports are used as a sales attraction by the firm. Typically, a report from one of them might be no longer than several paragraphs, topped by a set of figures showing earnings, ratios, and the like. Occasionally, if they are followers of one of the major glamour industries—the computer stocks or the oils, for example—they might be asked to turn out several pages, analyzing each major member of the industry. These are the people referred to by a Merrill Lynch vice-president, who said at a recent cocktail party that he didn't "know an analyst worth more than $12,000 a year." Many earn more than that figure, but $20,000 a year is considered good.

The second group of analysts send analyses of stocks to their institutional clients first, after which they put the analyses into print for distribution by the firm to individuals. Until they were forbidden by the SEC and the Stock Exchange, "giveups" (an under-the-table sharing of commissions by brokers) went to many of the analysts in this group, as directed by the institutions paying the commissions.

The third group of analysts is characterized more simply. These are the ones who do not *send* analyses but *telephone* their favored clients, generally institutions and individuals with large investments in the market, and write their reports for general distribution *after* finishing their phone reports. As might be expected, such analysts are not men and women clandestinely operating behind a locked door but often the most important members of the firm—for example, the partner in charge of research.

It is not hard to understand why analysts try to build up a private clientele. Most are poorly paid. They are the first to be fired in market breaks such as those of 1962 and 1969–1970. Between October, 1969 and October, 1970, over four hundred of the Street's 2,700 analysts were laid off as the result of the bear market. Many are also paid according to their "production," that is, according to the degree they generate trading and commissions for their firms. In fact, the production of many analysts is the deciding factor in annual salary reviews. Only rarely are they appraised on the value or the substance of their reports, for in Wall Street all that counts is the generation of money. With such little protection it is no wonder that the typical analyst is concerned less with the public and more with the big trader.

Some analysts, of course, build a major following, and their output will warrant a partnership, and they may share in the excessive profits Wall Street chalks up. Indeed, any man who has been named the partner in charge of research of a Wall Street firm may be considered to have achieved his position by virtue of having an investment following of some size.

But some of the biggest chunks of income that analysts take home are under-the-table commissions paid them by mutual funds and other institutions—not for "buy" but for "sell" information. Since most brokers duck sell advice, a thriving sort of black market has developed for the analysts. The result has been a strengthening in the trend among certain analysts to be more responsive to their institutional clients' wishes than to those of the regular customers of their firms. In fact, the basic allegiance of many analysts is not to their firms but to the institutions they deal with under the table. So rampant is this dealing that it has led institutions to wonder how many other major traders have already been notified when they hear from their favorite black market analyst.

Still, the big investors do have the assurance that they will be *called*. The small investor is *never* called. He must wait until the analyst's words are in print and a general distribution is under way. This means he is the last to learn the analyst's latest thoughts. By the time word does filter down, the privileged institutional and individual clients have already taken their positions in a stock or sold out and taken their profits— just as the small investor buys in.

7

The back offices

It was in 1968 that Wall Street's back offices collapsed. That collapse showed perhaps better than anything else why the Street was unfit to regulate itself, for the collapse was the result of complete abdication of the responsibility that accompanies self-regulation. Literally, the firms took the money of their customers and failed to deliver what had been paid for, that is, securities. Many did so knowing full well they could not deliver.

The New York Stock Exchange blamed unexpected trading volume for the collapse, but the truth lay elsewhere. The sharply higher trading of fifteen million shares a day or more didn't just happen. It was the result of a vast Wall Street selling effort led by the Exchange itself. The effort had never before been equaled. At the same time, it was the result of the greed of men who were basically small-time entrepreneurs. While the dollars poured into the front offices of Wall Street's brokers and partners and salesmen took more than their fair share of profits, the back offices, where the stock transaction was literally carried out, received little development money, few additional personnel, and practically no direction from management at the highest levels.

Indeed, Wall Street's back offices more often than not resembled the depressing sweat shops of another day. Furnishings were sparse, and the few hand-me-down tables, desks, and files that were provided nearly always were chipped, cracked, and in dire need of paint. Wages were low, as little as $60 a week for some low-level people, and overtime and even night work became mandatory as trading volume built.

For reasons that have never really been clear, most back office workers resisted campaigns to unionize until the late 1960s, when most workers joined up in a rush. It is ironic that before then many felt that seeking union membership would be a disloyal act. Working in Wall Street gave others vicarious thrills. A great many, perhaps the majority, interpreted the loose reins of their employers as permission for a kind of social anarchy in the office. Many file cabinets, for example, were stocked with liquor for that unexpected birthday, wedding, engagement, or leaving-for-a-better job party. Even at the Stock Exchange, an impromptu party could be organized in minutes; the elegant board of governors room was always available for the senior staff parties. Moreover, most offices in the Street were ready on short notice to bombard astronauts, ballplayers, politicians, and other assorted celebrities with ticker tape, teletype printouts, business forms, toilet paper, and vital investment records—including some suspect, stock certificates.

When the New York Mets baseball team won the World Series, the downpour of paper from the Exchange incited the board of governors to take the unusual step of sending a chastising memo to the staff rather than leaving it to the Exchange administration. The tons of paper that fell into the streets that day made walking a hazard, while the toilet paper wrapped around the steeple of Trinity Church, though it brought chuckles to some, had to be stripped away by firemen at a risk to their lives. (In the pandemonium, someone walked into the Morgan Guaranty and stole $13 million worth of securities.) In contrast, a great many Wall Street partners saw the back office galas as the simple venting of high spirits and even honest patriotism, as in the case of parades for astronauts. The galas helped to compensate for the inadequate salaries and fringe benefits, and no one—New York officials or Wall Streeters—made any fuss.

As might be expected, the working conditions of the back offices attracted a particular segment of the New York population. Few back office workers were well educated; many were not very intelligent or ambitious. They were recruited from the outlying boroughs of the city, and many were hired from Mafia-controlled employment agencies, as was revealed by J. Mitchell Graybard, director of personnel and training for Smith, Barney & Company at a Security Control Conference held in New York in November, 1969. Even these people looked on Wall Street's back offices as no place to work for long; turnover rattled along at 60 percent a year,

Though most back office employees do not work directly in it, their working days revolve around a nineteenth century anachronism called the *cage*. It is in the cage that a firm sorts out incoming and outgoing stocks and accepts deliveries from and makes them to its customers, other brokers, banks, and, if the particular house is one of the Exchange's 285 clearing brokers, the Stock Clearing Corporation, which is owned and operated by the Exchange.

The cage's work is complicated largely because, from the time someone somewhere sells a stock to the time a buyer somewhere else receives a new certificate, seventy-five to a hundred manual operations have to be performed. Nearly all require the filling out of a piece of paper, and nearly all the chores are carried out by back office people. The cage's work is crucial in still another way. It is the place where the stock trade is consummated. The work carried out in the cage is what brokers are paid for, and it has to be carried out within deadlines as short as one-half hour for some cash stock trades and never more than four days.

In a time of light trading volume, say, 2 or 3 million shares a day, the cage worked well enough. In the 1960s, however, when 12-million-share days were routine and volume went as high as 20 million shares on some days, the cage as a system for processing stock trades fell apart.

When the breakdown came, the extent of the chaos was hard to imagine. Physically, the scene in many back offices raised the image of a public toilet in which paper towels had been tossed everywhere. In the case of back offices, however, the scattered papers too often were stock certificates.

Among the people working in the offices, the capacity for error, carelessness, and theft was limitless. Stock certificates were left for weeks piled haphazardly on any level surface—on filing cabinets, behind which the certificates occasionally fell, or on tables, from which they were often brushed into waste baskets. Stocks sent to investors were mailed to wrong addresses or not mailed at all. An investor who bought 100 shares might receive 1,000—or 100 shares of a different stock, a bond, or just an empty envelope. A man in Pennsylvania wrote the Exchange that the monthly statement his broker was sending him credited him with owning a $1 million worth of bonds, and he couldn't get the statement corrected.

For those investors who chose to leave stocks with their brokers for safekeeping, the list of troubles was just as diversified. Monthly statements were credited with stock never bought or with the wrong number of shares. A customer of McDonnell & Company, for example, bought 300 shares of stock in Technitrol, Inc. The man paid cash for his purchase and asked that the certificates be delivered to him. Months went by, and though the man had called the management of McDonnell's, it was only after he enlisted the aid of the Stock Exchange that delivery was made. Meanwhile, each month's statement carried the notation that he was the owner of 300 shares of stock in Fuqua Industries, although he had never made such a purchase. Compounding the inaccuracy was the fact that never once did it carry a notation that he was the owner of 300 shares of Technitrol.

Technitrol was a company that paid no dividends, so this particular stock purchaser was spared additional agony—that of getting the brokerage firm to credit him with dividends rightfully his. Unless investors who left their securities with brokers kept track of dividends due, chances were that they would never be credited with them. Many did not keep track, and many lost hundreds of dollars. Dividends, both cash and stock, often were mailed or credited to former share owners, who refused to return them when the mistakes were discovered; the new owners, though entitled to the dividends, did without.

In 1968, when the Exchange had just begun to organize a depository for stocks owned or held by brokers for their customers and had taken responsibility for distributing dividends, the Exchange was unable to deliver $4 million in dividends. Thus snarled were the records of such companies as McDonnell & Company, Goodbody & Company, Hayden, Stone—indeed of some fifty firms.

How much of this confusion was caused by sheer incompetence may never be known. Many mistakes were not mistakes at all but theft by employees, as shown earlier in *Fleecing the Lambs,* who used the general collapse as a cover for their activities.

Despite new, protective measures such as employee fingerprinting, the hiring of private guards and detectives, and more intensive screening of employees' backgrounds, thefts continue on a large scale.

Time and again in 1970 Wall Street brokers reported large thefts traced to the back office. In December, 1970, for example, a back office supervisor for Scheinman-Hochstein & Trotta was indicted and charged with involvement in the theft of $2.3 million worth of securities.

Bad as back office thefts were for Wall Street, an even greater threat—since the Street's very survival is at stake—is the failure of brokers to deliver stock to each other.

The heart of a stock transaction is the transfer of title to a buyer at the time he makes payment. A crucial step in this process, obviously, is the physical delivery of stock from the seller's broker to the buyer's broker. It is at this point, too, that the buyer's broker pays for the stock.

The clearing operation of the New York Stock Exchange's Stock Clearing Corporation reduces the need to deliver stocks physically by about 30 percent. In clearing, a member's total purchases and sales in a stock during a single day are matched against each other, and only the net balances are physically delivered and received. But the 70 percent of daily volume that requires delivery threatens to close down Wall Street. Without stock certificates, the stock transaction—the trade, the investment, whatever one chooses to call it—cannot be made.

This inability to deliver stock certificates between brokerage firms is called "fails," and by 1968 the fails rate was high indeed. Early in that year the value of the stock that brokers had failed to deliver to each other was *$2.5 billion*. By December it went to $5.1 billion, and it stayed there through January, 1969. As much as $750 million worth of securities were thirty days or more behind in delivery, and many were six months behind. It is beyond the imagination of any layman to envision the backup this created. It can be understood, however, that every dollar represented a debit against firms who had not made deliveries, and it was many of those with the greatest fails pileup that ultimately went out of business or were forced to merge (Goodbody & Company, F. I. duPont, and Hayden, Stone). In 1969, the fails level dropped from a high of over $4 billion to about $1.4 billion not because of any newly found efficiency among Wall Street's brokers but because the 1969 bear market was taking hold, and trading volume had dried up.

Though $1.4 billion is not peanuts, some of the first people to be laid off as the result of the bear market were back office employees, partly because there are those in Wall Street who think $1.4 billion a tolerable figure. Among them was Eugene

Miller, the Exchange's own vice-president for public relations and advertising. In the spring of 1969, Miller hastily ordered advertising campaigns proclaiming that the "paper work problem," a euphemism to describe the back office collapse, had been solved. In one campaign he succeeded in persuading *Business Week* magazine to agree to publish a twelve-page advertising supplement in which eleven pages were to be bought by firms and corporations to endorse Miller's single page of copy. Clearly thinking of the repercussions if the assertions proved untrue and also sensitive to comments from Washington, Exchange president Robert Haack vetoed that campaign and a similar one Miller had planned for the *Wall Street Journal.*

The Exchange's own publications and its news releases thumped hard for claims that the Exchange could not hope to substantiate. Many of these claims, nevertheless, were picked up by newspapers and magazines. Wall Street, the Exchange releases said, was spending $100 million on automating paper work, though no bona fide survey of such spending had ever been undertaken. One release said that the paper work problem was "coming to an end," but this was not a fact. Another said that the securities industry in mid-1969 was capable of handling 24,000,000 shares a day; the statement must have sent shivers down the spines of some of the responsible men in Wall Street, including Haack's.

If the optimism was unwarranted, it is true that one practical accomplishment in those days of high fails and mendacity was the mid-1968 revival of a ten-year-old plan for cutting into back office paper work. Called Central Certificate Service (CCS), the plan was basically sound, but it had been shelved because of opposition from the board of governors to spending money on what was, after all, only the back office. The idea behind CCS was to establish a stock depository featuring a vault and a computer located in the sub-basement of 44 Broad Street, at one time the address of the *Wall Street Journal.* Its goal, as stated by Lee D. Arning, vice-president of the Exchange's operations when CCS was started in 1968, was a reduction by 75 percent of physical certificate handling. Title to stocks would be transferred electronically.

In fact, CCS managed to immobilize great numbers of securities. At first deposits were kept in the CCS vault, but after an extensive manual counting by squads of Exchange employees, the deposits were converted to certificates of large denominations and sent to custodial banks. Meanwhile, the depositors of stock were able to order delivery of shares to other depositors by instructing CCS to make the appropriate computer bookkeeping entries. In theory, CCS seemed to be the answer to Wall Street's back office shambles. In practice it turned out to be something else.

By the end of 1969, while CCS had just under half a billion shares on deposit valued at $25 billion, the market value of stocks traded in October alone was $661.4 *billion,* and 15 billion shares were listed for trading by year's end. Nor were all of Wall Street's brokers CCS depositors. Only those firms engaged in clearing operations used the CCS vault.

CCS did not even start out well. In its first weeks, it was inundated with stocks because the Exchange failed to establish a coordinated delivery system, and the sub-basement of 44 Broad Street resembled the worst kind of back office imaginable. The scene consisted of a large room full of tables on top of which stock certificates were piled. Many remained there for weeks, for, like its member firms, the Exchange had gone to the same back office labor market to find people to count the certificates and the number of shares they represented. The salary offered was as little as $60 a week. Besides, many people who answered the Exchange's employment advertisements fled after a day or two, if not at once, and the Exchange was forced to call in its regular office force to count stocks.

All the while security and supervision were lax, at best, though CCS, in the words of the Exchange, was designed "with maximum security in mind." One Exchange employee, a woman who had been drafted for duty with CCS, remarked afterward how easy it would have been for anyone working there to slip a handful of stock certificates into a handbag. All that kept many from doing just that was ignorance of the negotiability of the stock certificates they were handling. Few checks are run on the people who have physical control of certificates, and many a Wall Street back office thief has turned stolen certificates over to a bank as collateral for a personal loan. Often, certificates are sold at branch offices of Wall Street brokers, away from New York and often in foreign countries. Clearly, even the exchange had no control, either, for as late as mid-1971 seven employees of CCS were charged with stealing $2.6 million worth of stock in Walt Disney Productions, Duke Power Co., and IBM.

A scarcity of help and the constant threat of theft were not all that dogged CCS, however. Several times in a day, the Exchange computers—nine IBM 360/50s—to which CCS was linked, literally stopped. The trouble lay not with CCS or its programming but with the Exchange's $3.5 million electronic data processing system. Although in three years Haack had fired two vice-presidents in charge of the Electronic Systems Center (one of whom he had hired himself) and had put responsibility for its overall operation on R. John Cunningham, his executive vice-president, the system continued to operate badly, falling down even on simple payroll processing. CCS was just another of its victims.

While on the one hand, CCS never solved the chaos of the back offices—in the spring of 1971, with a major rise in the market under way, fails rose ominously to nearly $1 billion among only sixty-three firms—on the other hand, it was the only solution the Exchange proposed. A single, vast depository used by *everyone* was the answer—to the Exchange, at least. Yet CCS was hardly regarded as a universal solution. Most banks, for example, had a stock processing backup as big as Wall Street's brokers', but many were reluctant to join CCS for two reasons—both evident before CCS was introduced though neither was taken into account in the Exchange's planning.

First, banks were anxious to see the stock certificate eliminated in favor of a machine-readable certificate (something like a check), and they had invested in paper-handling and data-processing equipment that was geared, in the long run, to this. Second, laws and regulations governing the banks' fiduciary responsibility prohibited them from turning over to the Exchange the safekeeping of securities entrusted to them.

Eventually First National City Bank agreed to join the CCS stock processing system in 1970, but even then it was not prepared to deposit stocks with it. The bank agreed only to receive and deliver securities through a CCS account, which was closed out at the end of each day's trading.

First National, other banks, and even institutional investors blocked by laws and regulations from joining CCS may become members one day, though, for the Exchange is working to change the laws through lobbying and through campaigns aimed at influential groups such as the American Bar Association. One change, which would amend the Investment Company Act of 1940, would allow banks to deposit securities they hold as custodians for mutual funds and closed end investment companies. The amendment would let the bank, acting as custodian, or the funds and investment companies themselves make the deposits.

Another change sought by the Exchange would occur in the regulations of the Comptroller of the Currency governing trust accounts and pension funds. Each trust and pension fund account must at present be kept separate from all other accounts by their custodians and must be under the control of two bank offices. Each trust account and each fund must be separately identifiable. Lumped into CCS, this would not be possible except through receipts and bookkeeping entries—changes the Exchange is lobbying for.

The changes in regulations that the Exchange is seeking obviously must be approached with more than usual caution. A system of trading stocks that depends on receipts and bookkeeping requires proficient and honest management. Wall Street has demonstrated that it does not overflow with this element. The stock certificate is a tangible asset. A receipt merely indicates the existence of an asset. The bankruptcy in the early 1960s of Ira Haupt & Company was caused by the firm's naive acceptance of receipts for salad oil that never existed. In that insolvency, the Exchange paid out $9.5 million in cash to 3,870 securities customers and delivered $490 million in securities to the firm's customers, as well.

The insolvency led the Exchange to establish its Special Trust Fund. But it also underscored the perils of permitting brokers to mingle the cash of their customers, that is, the so-called free credit balances, with the brokers' own. In fact, the Haupt scandal taught Wall Street little. The Exchange's Special Trust Fund of $55 million was exhausted by early 1971, as was another $20 million added to it in January of that year. By then only the creation by Congress of the Securities Investor Protection Corporation, which insures brokerage customers up to $50,000, seemed an adequate solution to cash and securities losses caused by brokers' failures.

It is paradoxical in the extreme to note that when Representative Emmanuel Celler, a Republican from New York and chairman of the House Judiciary Committee, called for a special study of how brokers used the free credit balances of customers for their own purposes, the House rejected the idea. Its Commerce Committee, which is chaired by Harley Staggers, Democrat of West Virginia, said that free credit balances would be part of an investigation that would examine "substantial questions," especially those of self-regulation. In the meantime, let the buyer beware—and hold his stock certificates.

8

Wall Street's salesmen

ON November 14, 1968, the agenda of the weekly meeting of the Exchange's board of governors seemed to contain the usual items. Hoover Ball & Bearing wanted to list over 3.8 million shares for trading. Motorola International Development wanted to list $30 million worth of convertible debentures. A securities firm named Sassower, Jacobs and Schneider had applied for membership, and R. John Cunningham, the Exchange's executive vice-president, was to report on the growing failure of Wall Street's firms to deliver securities to each other.

Midway through the agenda, however, an item of business appeared that was turning up with ever greater frequency—an appeal by a securities salesman who had been disciplined by the Exchange's Department of Member Firms.

In this case the salesman was Michael DuBroff, an employee of A. L. Stamm & Company. DuBroff had been censured and suspended from employment for three months by the Conduct Division of the Department of Member Firms for a fairly common practice. For two years during the height of bull market trading and mounting back office confusion, DuBroff had allowed a favored customer to buy stocks and pay for them only *after* they had been sold. James R. Foster, Jr., a margin clerk, had known of DuBroff's activities but had failed to report them. The clerk was consequently suspended for one month. DuBroff's supervisor, a branch office manager named Charles Lowlicht, also was suspended for three months and was denied a supervisory job with any Exchange firm until August 1, 1970. Lowlicht, in the Exchange's view, had "permitted DuBroff to service an account which for two years was meeting payment by liquidation." Lowlicht also had asked Foster, the clerk, to keep silent until he, Lowlicht, had "straightened out the account."

The DuBroff appeal to the Exchange's board of governors was heard first by the board's advisory committee, which also considered letters written on DuBroff's behalf by Donald G. Fern, a manager, and Malcolm J. Babbin, a partner of A. L. Stamm. Despite the letters, the advisory committee recommended that the board uphold the original penalty—which it did.

The DuBroff case was a single incident among tens of thousands, possibly hundreds of thousands, that occurred in the bull markets of the 1960s. DuBroff's crime, which in the eyes of most of his fellows was that he had been caught, demonstrates the loose ethics and downright dishonesty that are to be found among firms regulated by the New York Stock Exchange. It also demonstrates the type of slap-on-the-wrist penalties that the securities industry's self-regulators mete out.

Under cover of rampaging stock trading volume and collapsed back offices where records were a shambles, securities salesmen revived a variety of manipulative and deceptive practices not seen to any great extent since the 1920s. Many ignored the temperament, resources, and goals of their investor–customers and sold them stocks not suited to them. Many widows and orphans were put into high flying conglomerates that came crashing down when the inevitable correction came in 1969 and 1970. Even intelligent, astute investors were put into issues, particularly in the over-the-counter market, that should not even have been approved for public trading.

Salesmen churned accounts and made trades without authorization by their customers. They put customers into slow moving new issues that were gathering dust on the shelf, charging no commissions—as is usual in new issue distributions—but collecting *double* commissions from the issuing corporations. If a new issue was considered "hot," salesmen often kept their allotment for themselves, in a practice called free-riding, or distributed it to relatives or favored customers. If a new issue or one already in public hands seemed lukewarm in terms of demand, brokers, acting also as dealers in the over-the-counter market, resorted to an old manipulative pricing practice known as "pegging"—in which the broker–dealer provides bid and ask quotations that have little relation to demand. In the markets for listed stocks, the Exchange warned salesmen against "painting the tape," a practice in which organized groups buy and sell a stock in order to create the illusion of activity, consequently creating interest among legitimate investors.

The practices of many salesmen did not stop at "violating principles of trade," a euphemistic phrase used by the Exchange to describe some salesmen's manipulative practices. Exchange records show that many salesmen violated not only securities laws but common law as well. For example, in February, 1970, the Exchange disclosed that Joseph Gold, a securities salesman from Brooklyn, had used the accounts of customers to steal funds from his firm. Gold, who was a margin clerk as well as a salesman, ordered a check drawn on his firm in his wife's name. Then he debited a customer's account for the same amount. Next he credited the same customer's account to cover the debit and debited a second customer's account. Besides being denied further employment of any kind by any Exchange firm, Gold faced criminal charges, was found guilty, and was placed on probation by a New York court for one to three years.

In January, 1970, the Exchange said that another New York salesman, Richard H. Milk, had bought stocks in the same manner as Michael DuBroff: that is, he paid for them only after he had sold them. Unlike DuBroff, however, Milk bought the stocks for himself, not for a customer. At times Milk also paid for securities with worthless checks, and at other times he requisitioned checks from his customers' accounts to pay personal bills.

Significantly, the shenanigans of salesmen turned up everywhere in the United States. In Paducah, Kentucky, a salesman named William L. Hardy promised a bank 500 shares of a stock as collateral for a personal loan. Hardy, who did not have the collateral, nevertheless wrote a letter to the bank on his firm's stationery saying that the stock was in transfer and would be delivered by the firm as soon as it was received. He signed the letter with the name of an employee in his firm's cashier department.

A Philadelphia salesman, Anthony Di Dio, pledged the securities of a customer for personal loans to buy real estate. In San Francisco, salesman Liam J. Bergin ordered a check drawn on an investor's account; he endorsed it and deposited it in his personal checking account. A Seattle salesman, Charles T. Lundell, gave a worthless check to his employer to pay for securities he had bought. Then, after his employer had found out and had restricted his trading, the salesman began trading through the account of another salesman in the firm.

The most prevalent and widespread practice of salesmen is churning the accounts of their customers. Thousands upon thousands of cases have been documented in the files of the exchanges and the SEC, and undoubtedly hundreds of thousands more instances have never come to light. Churning is not always so obvious as in the case of Beverly Hill salesman Harry Gliksman. On September 19, 1969, the New York Stock Exchange suspended Gliksman from working for any Exchange member firm for six months. Gliksman had churned a customer's securities to the extent that turnover had reached 43.7 percent in the customer's margin account and 12 percent in his cash account. Gliksman claimed he had been given verbal discretion by the customer, but he knew full well that the rules required the customer's written authorization. But even with written authorization the orders Gliksman executed for the account were excessive in frequency, especially in the light of the customer's modest resources.

Salesmen will defend churning, illegal and unethical though it is, as something they are forced into. Paid on a straight commission basis, they are hardly disinterested observers of customers' accounts. Nor are they likely to be good investment advisers. "Put us on a straight salary and give us a bonus now and then for being good managers, and maybe churning will stop or be reduced," says one customer's man. This may or may not be the answer, but salesmen now take greater risks than ever when they churn accounts, for customers are beginning to strike back through the courts.

Not long ago a New York resident, Guy R. Pierce, opened an account with C. B. Richard, Ellis & Company. Pierce's investment funds were modest in size—$3,000 in all. But in one month, as it was later described by a judge of New York's civil court, "Fifteen purchases of a single security were made in the plaintiff's account aggregating over $31,000, and sales of the same security were made during the same period of time aggregating more than $26,000." For churning the account, the brokerage charged Pierce commissions of $1,022, and it reduced his $3,000 stake to $110.98 in cash and securities worth $50! At one point his broker bought and sold short the *same stock in the same day* and managed to lose money both ways. As put by the judge, who returned Pierce's money to him, "Horses would have given the plaintiff a fairer opportunity to realize on his investment."

Investors whose accounts have been churned do not always complain, much less go to court. Even when they do complain, they frequently settle for the most superficial explanation. In the District of Columbia, for example, broker Philip B. Seidel

traded the accounts of five customers without their authorization. Eventually one of the customers objected, but he seemed
satisfied (he stopped writing and calling) after the broker typed
on a confirmation slip, "This is a canceled order." In fact it
was not canceled, as the customer's monthly statement eventually showed.

Tales of loose ethics and downright dishonesty are endless,
as official records of the Stock Exchange and the SEC show. It
is practically a daily occurrence for each to release reports of
brokers' suspensions, fines, and firings. At the Exchange, the
notices are distributed from the Department of Member Firms
in an almost monotonous string with the heading, "Subject:
Disciplinary Action."

Even more important documentation are the hundreds of
thousands of letters written by investors complaining of an
enormous variety of misdeeds by securities salesmen. The
letters go to the Exchange, the firms, the salesmen themselves,
and even to the press. At the Exchange, thousands are received,
sometimes hundreds in a single day, but only a handful (285 in
1969, for example) are considered serious enough for the Exchange to apply penalties. Some become the basis for initiating
Exchange investigations, which result in the kinds of hearings
and token penalties mentioned earlier. Many complaints are resolved with telephone calls to the offending salesmen and their
firms, and in such cases no punitive measures are taken by the
Exchange. Punishment is often left to a branch manager, who
may discipline the man under him by taking him to lunch.

Letters can occasionally result in a major investigation,
though usually only if they go to the SEC. In 1969, for example,
when still in business, McDonnell & Company began pitching
its customers a stock called Waltham Industries. The company
was one that McDonnell salesmen likened to a conglomerate—
one that was just being born. After being sold to McDonnell
customers at prices ranging from $45 to $55, the stock plummeted within a few weeks to the low thirties, then went still
lower. It finally got into the teens. Letters from irate McDonnell customers to the SEC caused the first wave in what de-

veloped into a full-scale investigation of McDonnell salesmen —seventeen in all—who, their supervisors attested, said things about the Waltham stock that just weren't true. Besides questioning the brokers involved, the SEC sent each buyer of the stock a questionnaire with the aim of determining how McDonnell salesmen had persuaded their customers to make the purchase.

Most letters, of course, do not lead to investigations. Most are simply ignored, especially those sent to brokerage firms. Even at the Exchange many complaints go unanswered, possibly because management at the highest level early in 1968 pinned the label, "idiot mail," on written complaints. The rest of the senior staff take their cues from that.

At the member firms salesmen are required by the Stock Exchange to take complaints promptly to their branch managers for investigation; the managers are required to hear out the aggrieved customer. In recent years, though, most managers have sprung aggressively to the defense of salesmen and given "short shrift to the customer," as an Exchange-published booklet said, especially when customers felt they were given bad investment advice and were touted into buying stocks that went down in price. The booklet, verbosely titled *Supervision and Management of Registered Representatives and Customer Accounts,* is a guide for branch office managers. It instructs them to investigate complaints "in their initial stages" since the complaints "are, in fact, being registered against his direction of his office. Certainly tact is essential," the booklet continues, "even when the customer is wrong." Too often the branch manager and his salesmen have taken to heart only the last phrase.

Proving that a salesman gave a customer bad investment advice is difficult. In the case of Waltham Industries stock and the investigation by the SEC of McDonnell salesmen, the inquiry took two years. Conversations between a customer and a salesman are nearly always privately conducted by telephone, and in a dispute the salesman's word is usually taken by the branch manager before the customer's. The customer can appeal to the Stock Exchange, which will grant a hearing. But the offer is usually worthless since few customers can travel what may be thousands of miles to explain the wrong they've complained about. Most of the time the amount of money involved makes such travel impractical even if the wronged customer has the time.

Still, the mounting number of customer complaints cannot be ignored, and, reflecting its concern over salesmen's honesty as early as 1963, the Stock Exchange established a permanent staff to inspect sales offices—something it would hardly have done if salesmen had impeccable reputations. It also published and distributed among securities firms a variety of booklets that described securities laws and informed salesmen that they were required to observe those laws. The goals of ethical conduct, the Exchange said in one booklet, could be found in the Exchange's constitution—a document, the booklet suggested, comparable to the Declaration of Independence and the Constitution of the United States both in spirit and in purity of expression.

The entire editorial content of the booklet *Ethical Conduct,* the title of which clearly suggests its need, warned salesmen against fraudulent practices, boiler room operations, and stock manipulation. It pointed out, too, that the "relationship between a registered representative [the Exchange's euphemistic term for salesman] and the investing public was a solemn trust requiring unfailing adherence to the high standards of commercial honor and integrity." Specifically the booklet said that a salesman "must have both the desire and the competence to do what is best for his customers, his firm, and the industry and, therefore, what is best for himself."

As any securities salesman knows, this can be an irreconcilable set of goals. Most investors turn their stocks over infrequently, yet a salesman's income depends completely on his "production." If he persuades his customers to trade, he may be guilty of churning or at least of not operating in his client's best interest. If he does not generate trading, his own income will drop. In his own mind he clearly will not be doing what is best for himself, and he certainly will not be making his firm happy.

Most securities salesmen receive about one-third of the commissions they generate, though there are no hard and fast rules governing that rate. Some firms maintain a sliding scale, paying their "big producers" 40 to 50 percent. One method of computing a salesman's commissions involves determining the size of his average trade and basing his overall percentage on that. Nearly every firm maintains some kind of bonus system, both covert and open. Big ticket salesmen often prefer under-the-table cash payments instead of a high percentage. Some firms also pay bonuses based on the debit and credit balances in customers' accounts. Debit balances require a firm to borrow money to maintain those balances, but this is a profitable activity, since the firm passes the costs on to the customer— adding 15 to 20 percent profit for itself. Interestingly, such loans, which are nearly always made to margin account customers, are specifically exempted from the Truth-in-Lending Act, thanks to Exchange lobbying in Congress. As for credit balances, they, of course, give a firm access to money at no cost.

Securities left with firms in margin accounts can be used as collateral by the firm, while one or two dishonest houses have even used securities fully owned by customers. On June 16, 1970, for example, the Exchange fined and suspended Meyerson & Company of San Francisco and two of its officers, Harry Meyerson and D. Russell Burwell, for pledging customers' fully paid for securities on bank loans negotiated between November, 1969, and March, 1970.

A successful salesman earns $25,000 to $30,000 a year in Wall Street and a truly good one, by generating commissions totaling $100,000, can take home $40,000 or more. Some firms have percentage bonus plans, which might pay a salesman his commission plus a retroactive 5 or 6 percent upon reaching the $100,000 mark. Thus, instead of $40,000 in commisions, the salesman would make $45,000 or $46,000. A few—*very* few— salesmen manage to take home hundreds of thousands of dollars each year. Usually such salesmen have institutional accounts or rich individual customers who have given them discretion. The salesmen most people are likely to meet in Wall Street, however, earn far less. Wall Street, in fact, is heavily populated with men who make no more than $4,000 a year—perhaps because it is their first year in the business or because they are older men who have had to let down on the hard sell. Many firms also employ utility men or part-time salesmen, who, when demand requires it, must also carry out chores in the order room or the cage.

Some securities salesmen have been able to develop large incomes by bringing underwritings into their firms, though this is extremely difficult to accomplish. Others set up mergers between corporations or find acquisitions for growth-minded companies. The vast majority of salesmen, however, are still forced to rely completely on what is called retail commission business.

With only a few exceptions none of Wall Street's firms have attempted to solve the salesmen's conflict. A few—Merrill Lynch, for example—permit their salesmen to sell a broad range of investments—commodities contracts, rights, warrants, puts, calls, distributions of underwriting shares (for double commissions), and large blocks of stock called secondaries. To some extent, this relieves salesmen of the temptation to trade the securities accounts of their customers excessively.

The fact that most firms have done nothing to solve what is really a problem in management or to curb the shady practices of their salesmen is consistent, of course, with the way Wall Street's partners generally operate their businesses. Salesmen are seen only as "producers," men and women who generate income. Thus for years the firms tended to hire only the well connected, people whose friends and associates would become customers. Then, when the bull markets of the 1960s raised trading volume to extraordinary heights, the firms began to hire just about anyone who applied.

Regardless of their social and economic station, no matter how great their production, salesmen are usually held at arm's length by their employers. The relationship is, in fact, not so

much that of employer and employee as that of business connections. The firms merely provide facilities such as desk
space, telephones, a list of prospective customers, and investment research. There are no employee fringe benefits of any
consequence. In turn for being provided with a place to work,
salesmen are expected to generate enough money to make the
arrangement profitable for everyone.

Working under such conditions, most salesman go their own
way, a fact that helps to explain the widespread dishonesty and
the decline in ethical practices. Few develop loyalty to their
customers or to their firms. Job-hopping and pirating are
major problems for many securities firms not only because of
the administrative chores this presents to a firm or because
new salesmen have to be found constantly, but because a salesman who leaves usually takes his accounts with him. It is a
rare firm that possesses the marketing skills that enable it to
retain customers when salesmen leave for other firms. Only if
an account happens to be an institution paying large commissions will a firm try to keep a salesman by offering him better
facilities, a higher percentage of commissions, or even a
partnership.

It should be understood that most securities salesmen are
far from unhappy with the arrangements they have with brokerages. During the bull markets of the 1960s their incomes
matched and passed those of their firms' partners in many
cases. During the bear market and the back office failures, selling securities may have been an uphill effort, but all the while
the partners of many firms were losing millions in capital.

However, the same bear market produced a widening schism
between salesmen and their firms. The rift began to appear in
the spring of 1970, just after the Stock Exchange persuaded
the SEC to permit the levying of a $15 surcharge on stock
trades of 1,000 shares or less. When the firms and the Stock
Exchange decided to keep the entire $15, in effect reducing the
income of salesmen, the salesmen sued, charging that Wall
Street's firms and the Exchange had violated antitrust laws.

The suit, brought by the American Association of Securities

Representatives, an organization composed of 5,000 members, charged that the Exchange, the Association of Stock Exchange Firms, and forty-two brokerages had conspired to restrain trade by reducing the rates of commissions paid to securities salesmen.

The Exchange's response was that the surcharge was a labor matter, not an antitrust matter. A federal judge disagreed, saying that the securities salesmen were not an organized labor group and the suing association was not a labor union. Nor had there been any collective bargaining. For investors, the conflict had no meaning. The contestants had no real sympathy for the victims who were paying the surcharge. Just as pirates always have, the firms and the salesmen were fighting over the spoils.

Part 3

The Exchange

9

The members

ARLY in the spring of 1970, one of the Stock Exchange's most capable public relations writers pulled from his typewriter the final page of an article on which he had worked long and hard for *Nation's Business,* a magazine published by the U.S. Chamber of Commerce.

The writer, Lee Ehrenreich, was a disinterested, prolific professional who always had been able to transpose his understanding of the Exchange's various positions into prose that could be distributed publicly without embarrassment to the Exchange. He was also the writer of the Exchange's annual report, a task that indicated very well the extent of his talents since the all-important report must be written in a very special way.

Ehrenreich had found his assignment for *Nation's Business* difficult for two reasons, and he was writing under an enormous strain. First, the article was a ghosted piece, written to carry the by-line of Exchange President Robert W. Haack, who was often contemptuous of texts prepared for him by the public relations department. Second, the article was intended by the Stock Exchange to promote one of its most sacred themes—that self-regulation of the securities industry was good for everyone connected to it, *including* the customers. The title of the article was "Self-Regulation: How the Securities Industry Helps Customers—by Helping Itself." It was the intention of the Exchange to plant the piece in *Nation's Business*. A similar article was being prepared for publication in the *Wall Street Journal*.

The articles were part of a major image-making campaign in which the Exchange was trying to promote itself as a responsible regulator with a vital interest in public service. Some of the Exchange's senior staff, including Haack himself, probably felt that this was the way it should be. But the Exchange was as always an instrument of its member firms, so the truth was something else.

From its inception in 1792, the Exchange has been writing its rules solely for its members' benefit. Its limited objective, as stated by its constitution, has been to "furnish Exchange rooms for the convenient transaction of business by its members." It has never strayed far from that purpose. Non-members, including customers, have been viewed as outsiders, only permitted to buy securities through the members' monopoly and at substantial commissions.

Even after the optimistic reforms of the 1930s, the Exchange regulated and promoted the ownership of securities with the selfish interests of its members first in mind. The interests of everyone else—customers, non-member firms, and the general public—were secondary. Often, the question of public interest was mere camouflage of hidden motives. The ghosted articles suggested that the Exchange was a responsible regulator of its own industry. At the time, however, the Exchange was fighting for raises in minimum commissions—as high as 104.1 percent. Its arguments were keyed to a theme that the more brokers received for their services, the better their services would be.

No one bothered to call the Exchange on the obvious conflict, though it should have provoked a great deal of ridicule. It was no secret that the higher commissions that the Exchange confidently expected to be granted by September, 1970, were needed to save many of Wall Street's member firms from imminent insolvencies. It was widely known, too, that most firms, with or without higher commissions, were incapable of improving the service they gave to their customers.

The unfortunate truth is that despite the reforms of the 1930s, Wall Street is as avaricious as ever, and the Exchange is its most useful tool. Instead of being brutally overpowering in their treatment of customers, as they were in the twenties, the firms have become more sly, using the Exchange as the instrument through which they evade and ignore the public interest. The Exchange's record of proposing new rules and laws strictly in the public interest is slight. On the contrary, such proposals inevitably develop outside the industry—in particular within the SEC. The Exchange's stance has been reactionary and negative, confined nearly always to defending the narrow interests of its members.

The Exchange has never been above acting behind a facade of feigned public interest. In 1969 Congress was considering lengthening the six-months' period that securities had to be held in order to qualify them for long-term capital gains. As most investors know, long-term gains can be taxed at a maximum of only 25 percent; short-term gains, or those realized in less than six months, can be taxed at ordinary income rates, which run as high as 70 percent.

There were those in Congress who felt that by extending the long-term qualifying period, say from six months to a year, additional revenues for the government could be generated. Not so, said Donald L. Calvin, the Exchange vice-president whose major responsibility was lobbying in Washington and in state capitals, developing arguments for the members to repeat in speeches and conversations. In an unusual burst of concern for the small investor, Calvin argued that low- and middle-income groups would be the hardest hit since Exchange data suggested that they, rather than high-income groups, tended to take their gains in a period between six and twelve months of investment. Thus more and more people would be taxed at short-term capital gains rates if the change were made. Calvin failed to point out that most low- and middle-income earners hardly ever paid income taxes at a rate exceeding 25 percent; their incomes were simply not high enough, so it wouldn't matter much from a taxing point of view when they took their gains. On the other side of the coin, people in high-income groups were likely to delay the sale of securities until gains in them qualified for the lower capital gains rate of 25 percent. Thrown into a short-term category and thus treated as ordinary income, the gains could be subjected to the higher tax rates.

Although Calvin and the Exchange conveniently neglected to mention it, the high-income investors were the same people who generated large commissions; they bought and sold blocks of stock much larger than the low- and middle-income investor did. If they were to delay sales for tax reasons and become less active in the market, the incomes of brokers would suffer. It is not surprising that Calvin and the Exchange urged Congress to reduce rather than extend the long-term holding period, from six months to three months.

Feigned public interest and camouflaged arguments against capital gains tax reform strongly suggest the nature of the Exchange's character. Rather than a responsible regulator, the Exchange is a glorified *trade* association. And it has in that capacity created almost insoluble problems for itself. In 1966, the Exchange barred its member firms from dealing in Exchange-listed securities with non-member firms. The intention was to concentrate transactions in NYSE listings among member firms who charged the fixed minimum commission rates imposed by the Exchange. Enforcement of the rule (Number 394), however, brought real problems. Instead of receiving all the wealth for itself, the Exchange in its greed, encouraged the formation of third market firms who operate independently as brokers and dealers in Exchange-listed stocks.

Even for the most honorable and forward-looking men, the temptation would be great to maintain the monopoly of the Exchange and not to look beyond the present. Yet few men are so tempted. The Exchange rarely has been blessed with leaders who think beyond the "crowd" on the floor, of which they are a part, or the money generated by the Exchange monopoly. One must go back to the presidency of William McChesney Martin (1938–1941) to find someone who was above the crowd on the floor, someone who took public interest seriously. Most members and many leaders are men with a peddler's bent. Their language and bearing suggest quickly to observers that their only interest is to extract as much profit from their membership as possible. At the first sign of trouble, as in the 1969–1970 bear market, they sell their seats (sending the price of a seat down in 1970 from a high of $515,000 to a seven-year low of $170,000) and flee. Others withdraw their capital from their firms, forcing them into insolvency or near-insolvency. As described by the *New York Times*, "Practically every one of them is a small businessman, and almost all of them think small."

Throughout the Exchange's history the members have resisted strenuously any suggestion of change and have regarded any would-be reformer with an attitude that was sometimes vicious. Even the Exchange presidents felt the venom of their employers. For example, Keith Funston, who made many Exchange members rich, was regarded by those on the floor of the Exchange as a thorough-going WASP. White, Anglo-Saxon, and Protestant, Funston remained aloof, refusing even to learn the trading jargon of Wall Street. He was thoroughly disliked, and only his unmatched record of inducing millions of Americans to invest in securities allowed him to retain control.

The case of Robert W. Haack is another matter. Unlike Funston, Haack is an industry professional, with twenty-one years behind him as a broker and three as president of the National Association of Securities Dealers. However, Haack has made no one rich, and too many times he has voiced concern for the small investor. When he became president in

1967, the problems of the securities industry—its back office crush, insolvencies, the demands of institutions for membership—were already emerging, and Haack was considered the best man for the job. Not many months later, though, the members were spreading rumors that he wasn't able to handle the position.

Because of the self-interest of the Exchange's membership, it was inevitable that they would begin shooting at Haack. Most had had little to do with the average investor and arrogantly dismissed the mounting concern for him in Congress and in the SEC. A few of the Exchange's own figures suggest how ingrown were the interests of its members. In May, 1969, after the Exchange's annual classification of members according to function, it was discovered that only 759 out of 1,366 members, or little more than half the membership, did any public commission business at all. Among the remainder, 355 were specialists, making markets in stocks and trading for themselves; 109 were odd-lot dealers, also trading for themselves and doing a public business as well; 17 were floor traders, the real remnants of the private club; 78 were so-called two-dollar brokers; and 48 were inactive. These figures do not include the 5,600 or more nonvoting allied members, men and women who are partners or stockholders in the member firms.

Since more than half of the members dealt with the public to some extent, seemingly the public interest would be reflected in the one-vote-for-one-seat type of balloting common at the Exchange. But the number of members doing a public commission business is a figure as deceptive as any—though it is one, not surprisingly, that the Exchange chooses to publicize. Much more revealing is the extent of that business in each firm. The fact is that only a very few of the 759 had built any *substantial* business with the public. A great many of those counted dealt only with institutions, a kind of business that precludes any kind of allegiance to the millions of small investors.

The more reliable figures of the SEC show that fewer than 10 percent of the Exchange's 1,366 members accounted for more than 50 percent of the total public commission business. Conversely, more than half the seats on the Exchange were held by those members doing only 10 percent of the public commission business.

The fact that the Exchange's monopoly power lies with the members who trade for *themselves* can be confirmed by comparing voting power among firms with a large public commission business with those firms having none at all. Merrill Lynch is the undisputed leader of public commission business, yet in 1970 it held only seventeen seats and therefore had only seventeen votes. Paine, Webber, Jackson & Curtis, another firm with a very large commission business, held only eight seats and had only eight ballots in Exchange voting. At the same time, Wagner, Stott & Company, a specialist firm with *no* public business, controlled twelve seats and twelve votes. In ordinary balloting, insider's votes such as Wagner, Stott's would obviously never be cast in a way to further the public interest unless the public interest paralleled the insider interest—an unlikely occurrence. But there is no reason to believe, either, that those firms doing a large public business would necessarily become champions of the public interest if given more voice. For example, though Merrill Lynch was opposed to Exchange proposals to raise commission rates charged small investors, it made its opposing arguments in private talks. Publicly, it went along with the raise sought, saying merely that sharply higher rates should be avoided.

The Exchange's justification of the control of its insiders is that they play a crucial role in the continuance of the auction characteristic of the stock market, and that they keep it operating in an orderly fashion. However, it has been years since anyone with much knowledge of Wall Street has believed that old saw. The propaganda one has been exposed to has been labeled many times as nonsense, and a look at the members on the floor of the Exchange shows why.

Among the groups, the most controversial people have always been the specialists. In 1969 there were 355 of them. As members of eighty or more specialist units, each assigned an average of twenty stocks, they execute orders for others and maintain "fair and orderly" markets "insofar as reasonably practicable" the Exchange says. Specialists stabilize the market, the Exchange asserts, matching orders and selling short to supply buyers. In the face of public selling interest and receding prices, specialists buy to keep the market orderly and liquid: that amounts to unmatched sacrifice, the Exchange claims, since the specialists risk their own money. They are, the Exchange says in booklets, pamphlets, and statements to the press, responding—in the *public interest*—to the laws of supply and demand.

Regardless of statements issued by the Exchange, the *facts* are that time and again specialists have responded to other things. In 1962, when the market broke sharply, they responded to panic. They cut and ran, according to a special study of the SEC, which said the "specialists as a group did not have a significant stabilizing effect." Their panic was even greater in the twenty-seven minutes following the assassination of President Kennedy on November 22, 1963. During that time, more than 2.6 million shares were traded in the market, and the Dow-Jones average, a major market index, dropped over twenty-four points.

Because it feared the biggest decline in stock market history, the Exchange's board of governors cut the trading day short by eighty-three minutes. The board gave no hint, however, that the panic selling had been led by specialists dumping their shares, keeping one step ahead of the public. After an SEC investigation, Exchange President Keith Funston acknowledged that "not all specialists acted alike." Years later, in 1967, John A. Coleman, a former chairman of the Exchange's board of governors and a life-long specialist, described the reaction of the specialists on the day of the Kennedy assassination in a far more flattering light. "Everyone on the floor was stunned," Coleman said. You could feel the sense of personal loss. But they train interns to be doctors, and we've been trained to expect and deal with every crisis. And that's what we did."

The fact is that specialists have seldom performed well in a crisis—and for good reason. For years it has been clear that the capital of specialists, whether it is their own money or borrowed, has been insufficient to absorb selling waves. Indeed, the specialists have long been incapable of absorbing even the routine trades of institutional big blocks, and as far back as 1964, the SEC recommended an increase in the capital requirements of specialists.

Still, the inadequacy of specialists, the specialist system, and specialists' capital are only part of the controversy that surrounds these men. The other inadequacy involves questions concerning their adherence to basic ethical standards as they face the conflict of interest inherent in their positions. Besides making markets and determining the prices of stocks for the public, specialists are permitted to trade for themselves. Yet, though they account for as much as 30 percent of trading on the Exchange, the specialists' trades are *not* made public by being displayed on the Exchange's ticker tape. The specialist deals for himself in secrecy. Too often specialists have put their own interests ahead of others. Acting on inside bid-and-ask information only they possess, they have created trends in buying and selling not by reacting to *public* demand but by responding to threats to *their own* investment positions.

For instance, if a specialist feels his short position is too great, he might send a stock's price down, thus enabling himself to replace his shorted stock at a profit. If a specialist feels his long position is too great, he can just as easily send a stock's price up thus providing himself a tidy profit. Many specialists manipulate prices in their stocks to even out their own positions at the end of each day. Their "wipe-out" technique regarding stop orders was demonstrated in an earlier chapter.

The abuses of authority by specialists are well documented. According to SEC investigations, specialists have at times introduced stock buyers to brokers clearing for the specialists on the condition that the brokers kick back part of any commissions charged. Until the SEC exposed the practice in an investigation, thereby forcing the Exchange to prohibit it, the specialists had often accepted orders directly from personal friends and from executives of the corporations in whose stock the specialists made markets. In their transactions such customers inevitably received better prices than the public. At times, too, specialists who knew they would be assigned to make markets in particular stock issues bought shares directly from the corporation at low prices before the issue was listed. Indeed, specialists have even disclosed the extent of demand and supply, that is, orders to buy and sell, by disclosing the contents of their order books to favored brokers and others. This has occurred particularly in the distribution of secondaries —large blocks of stock a holder wishes to sell. The holder may be an underwriter, the corporation issuing the stock, an individual, or an institution. After learning the extent of bids entered in the specialist's book, the price of the secondary's shares are adjusted accordingly.

Such practices and the brawling, coarse, and irresponsible behavior of many specialists—few recognize a fiduciary responsibility, and some do not even know what it is—led the *New York Times* to describe the specialist in this way: "Unquestionably, he is the pig of the marketplace. His nose is dug in, and he cares for no one. His manner is crude and his speech ridiculously full of curses." That today's specialists are somewhat less awe-inspiring than those of yesterday is suggested by one of their own: "The basic auction market, with buyers and sellers bidding in front of the trading post, hasn't changed. The big difference, I guess, is that the men were of a different cut. They'd walk in with silk hats or derbies on their heads and striped trousers or black jackets. They had tremendous presence and could go into a crowd and dominate it just by the force of their personalities."

Nearly as controversial as the specialists are the floor traders, whose number has recently diminished from twenty in 1961 to seventeen in 1970. Floor traders undoubtedly hold the most privileged and selfish position in the stock market. They are free lances with no public contact at all. They make trades only for themselves and are the real speculators of the Stock Exchange since they roam the floor looking for quick profits.

In any balloting their votes automatically are cast for the preservation of the private club, for they are the last vestiges of that club. The Exchange has always defended the presence of floor traders, even to the extent of doctoring one of its own studies. In the mid-1960s the Exchange commissioned the consulting firm of Cresap, McCormick & Paget to develop material showing how the transactions of floor traders contributed to the market's liquidity. Unfortunately for the Exchange, the man who conducted the study, James Dowd, developed findings suggesting that floor traders were far from being the useful adjuncts to trading that the Stock Exchange said they were. The Exchange was aghast at the report and altered the results, Dowd maintained in public through newspapers, including the *New York Times,* and through the SEC. The SEC's commissioner at the time, William L. Cary, wanted to hold hearings, but in a full commission vote he was forced to accept the Exchange's version of the report.

The Exchange still says lamely that the transactions of floor traders contribute to the liquidity of the market. In a kind of a "poor-mouth" argument it also maintains that floor trading is hardly profitable because of the cost of transfer taxes on trades, clearing fees, and SEC fees—all of which are actually quite nominal. A floor trader would have to make three out of four trades advantageously, the Exchange maintains, to come up with a net gain.

Life is not actually that difficult for floor traders. They nearly always concentrate on the most active stocks, in which they may indeed add liquidity, but a sort of liquidity that is not needed. As hit and run artists, they are able to move in swiftly on their own to take advantage of situations, while investors are forced to find brokers to act for them. In the market breaks of the past ten years floor traders have actively participated by selling as the market fell and buying during runups. This, incidentally, is contrary to the Exchange's position. In defending the floor trader as someone whose buying and selling helps specialists make a continuous market, the Exchange describes him as a buyer during price declines and a seller during advances. This conceivably could be true but only when a floor trader is able to determine from his buddies, the specialists, that a turnaround is in the offing.

Floor traders trade for a mere fraction of the commissions levied on the general public. As holders of Exchange seats, they pay annual dues of $1,500 and contribute several hundred dollars a year to the Exchange's gratuity fund. That is about the extent of their cost of doing business on the New York Stock Exchange.

For years, the SEC demanded that floor traders accept specific duties when the public interest required it. The SEC regarded floor traders as scavengers whose activities upset the market's stabilization. As usual the Exchange saw the SEC's demands as a desire to usurp the self-regulatory function of the Exchange even though the SEC stated again and again that it desired to foment change from within, not to usurp the powers of the Exchange. In response, the Exchange invariably advised the SEC that it would do more for the public interest by concentrating on "other problems of the market."

The Exchange did make some changes in the rules governing floor traders: in 1964 it renamed them "registered traders" and required that 60 percent (later 75 percent) of their trades be "stabilizing transactions." It also forbade more than three of them to "be in the trading crowd for one stock at the same time." But the trouble was that the changes bypassed the central question: why are the floor traders there at all, operating only for themselves in the heart of the market with an obvious advantage over everyone else?

The other members of the Exchange—the two-dollar brokers and the odd lotters—have stirred little controversy, but in any showdown between insiders and the public they invariably vote on the side of the insiders.

Basically, the two-dollar brokers are free-lance agents who assist commission house brokers, handling trades for them at floor commission rates that used to be $2, hence the label, but were raised to $3.65 in 1970.

Like the $2 brokers, odd-lot members of the Exchange assist commission house brokers in executing orders. Unlike the $2 brokers, however, the odd-lotters are dealers themselves. Odd-lot trading has become the monopoly of a *single* firm, Carlisle DeCoppet & Company, as the result of a largely unnoticed merger in 1970 between the two firms that previously controlled the business: Carlisle & Jacquelin and DeCoppet & Doremus. Between them they accounted for 99 percent of the odd-lot dealings on the exchange.

Stationed in pairs at all of the Exchange's trading posts, odd-lot dealers of Carlisle DeCoppet (and associate brokers, who work for a fee) exercise orders for brokers at the 100-share, or round lot price determined by the specialists. Then they add from one-eighth to three-quarters of a point for themselves. As a result, investors who buy in odd lots pay an onerous number of costs. In addition to the regular commission and the surcharge paid to their broker, they pay the odd-lotter's fraction of a point, or differential.

The odd-lot business can be lucrative, but to what extent is known to only a few people. Like all Wall Street firms, Carlisle DeCoppet keeps its books a secret. Still, transactions have risen so sharply over the years, they suggest a flourishing and lucrative business. Between 1960 and 1968, Exchange figures show, annual transactions rose from 164.5 million to well over 300 million. Also, it is monopolized by one firm. Indeed, when the merger of Carlisle & Jacquelin and DeCoppet & Doremus was announced, one of the biggest fears of its partners—a fear presented to the Stock Exchange—was that there would be a reaction from the antitrust department of the U.S. Attorney General's office. However, Exchange management assured the firms there would be none, and indeed there wasn't. The government failed to announce why there was no investigation.

In recent years attacks on Exchange members have been growing sharply. As the shortsighted, narrow, selfish views, the incompetence, and the lack of capital have become understood publicly, they are no longer being tolerated. The insiders of the Stock Exchange, especially the men on the floor, are vestiges of another time. They have no place in a stock market so important to the well-being of the economy that upsetting its balance could easily hurl everyone into financial disaster, for the market is not only an indicator but a creator of economic well-being. Thus the SEC staff, if not its chairmen, have been conspicuously militant in dealing with Wall Street. Congress has demanded protection for investors, and hearings in 1971 were designed to disclose the extent of Wall Street's wrongdoing.

Indeed, by the end of 1970 even the Exchange members sensed that trouble was approaching. Though they chastised Robert Haack publicly for suggesting the need for change, the Exchange's board organized a panel to study its "governing, administrative, and voting procedures," and the men it chose to serve on the investigative panel were picked as much for their respectability as for any other quality. For the same reason the Exchange resurrected the most respectable figure ever associated with it to head the panel, William McChesney Martin. Seven months after his appointment, which he took at no pay, Martin said he was still a believer in self-regulation for the securities industry, but he also believed the SEC had to become "a sort of Federal Reserve Board," meaning there was need for far closer supervision. Martin also favored merging the Exchange with other trading centers and ending domination by floor members. He refuses, however, to consider cutting away the real cancer, self-regulation, for it is through this that any machinery, as witness his own reforms in the 1930s, can be subverted. Yet, the new reforms he suggests are an indication of Wall Street's own—albeit slight—response to a public opinion that has been turning against it for years now.

Many firms are very concerned with their image, especially since in March, 1970, they had voted overwhelmingly, 1,013 to

70, to change their constitution to enable them to sell stock in themselves—as corporations—to the general public. Once the decision was made and the firms went public, they would have to disclose more about their operations, including their financial status. In the light of such disclosures they would be forced to follow reasonably sound business practices.

It is no wonder that Wall Street was becoming responsive to outside pressures; there was much at stake. The shares of the one or two Wall Street firms that had gone public by the time the panel was formed were faring badly. For example, the shares of one of Wall Street's most successful institutional firms, Donaldson, Lufkin, Jenrette, had been introduced in the market in 1970 for $15 a share after the firm had discarded an offering price of $30 as too high. Late in 1970, bids for the stock in the over-the-counter market were as low as 9⅜. Even after an extraordinary runup of the market in the first six months of 1971, bidding for the firm's shares hovered around $13. If the shares had been listed on an Exchange, where prices generally are shaken down more severely, the bids would undoubtedly have been even lower.

How a firm's shares fared in the marketplace was not, however, of primary concern—except to those who had bought them—since no control was given up. Funds generated by the issues of Donaldson, Lufkin & Jenrette and by Merrill Lynch, which sold stock publicly in itself in July, 1971, was "found money." Thus, public ownership not only would generate funds, but *suggest* to Congress and other critics that the private club aspect of the Exchange had finally come to an end. Of course, the suggestion is not substantiated by fact since the same men will remain in charge. Indeed, the old rulers will become more powerful since they will be working with a far greater—and therefore more potent—base of capital. Once again the Exchange is arranging matters so that the public will continue to bail Wall Street out of a tight and threatening situation.

It is not hard to understand why the Exchange's firms are scrambling to hang on. The Exchange controls the movement of wealth so vast it is impossible for most people to imagine. The market value of the more than fifteen billion shares listed on the Exchange at the beginning of the 1970s was over $700 billion. During 1970, trading volume averaged over three hundred million shares a month, and in 1971 the average monthly volume will probably go well beyond this figure.

In turning over this volume, the "handle" of the firms has been $800 million in a year, while the cost of Exchange membership has been relatively low. A seat on the Exchange during the past several years has cost as much as $515,000, but many members purchased theirs when prices were considerably lower. The Exchange itself does not cost its members very much to operate; it is largely self-supporting. In 1968, the Exchange's expenses were budgeted at $45,515,500. Its revenues were budgeted at $50,598,500, or $5,083,000 more than expenses. The expectations of revenue, as the Exchange's figures show, were not unduly optimistic. By June 30, 1968, total revenue was running ahead of expectations by 14.3 percent. At the same time expenses were only 95.2 percent of what had been budgeted.

One of the main causes of the soaring revenue was an increase of 230.9 percent in fees paid by newly listing corporations. On the other hand, expenses declined for a simple reason: the Exchange decided not to introduce rate reductions for ticker and quotation services.

On the same date, June 30, 1968, the members' equity in the Exchange was $59,473,400, $6,209,500 more than the previous year. The figure included $27,157,200 (up from $23,-907,700) held in U.S. government securities for construction of a new building, which sum was later lumped in with the Exchange's special trust fund of $10,780,600.

At the time the Exchange merged its building fund with the special trust fund in the spring of 1970, it agreed to advance to New York City as prepayment on a land lease, enough money ($9 million) for the city to create a land-filled site in the East River at the foot of Wall Street.

Today those plans, which included a huge trading hall, may

be all but dead, for that sort of trading, with its crowds of shouting brokers, is a thing of the past. It may be only a short time before all trading is carried on by clicking, whirling electronic machinery that plays no favorites and resists corruption.

10

The Board of Governors

I N November, 1970, after President Robert Haack had suggested in public that the Exchange drop some of the trappings of the private club it still was, the response of the Stock Exchange's board of governors couldn't have been frostier. The Exchange, Haack said, ought to scuttle the high minimum commission rates, that shielded brokers, in favor of negotiated rates, at least on the big trades of institutions, and thus relieve the Exchange of a threatening problem: the demand for membership by mutual funds wishing to save money on commissions. The Exchange, Haack continued, ought to give member firms doing a large business with the general public—for example, Merrill Lynch and Bache & Company—more influence in Street affairs. (At the time Haack spoke there was not a single Merrill Lynch man on the board of governors.) Haack suggested that the listed corporations also be given some authority. Wall Street patsies that they were, U.S. corporations paid enormous fees to the Exchange for listing their shares, and they toed financial marks that the Exchange would never have dreamed of setting for its own often shaky and sometimes crooked member firms.

In the board's view, as expressed by its chairman, Bernard J. Lasker, the Haack supplications were heresy, for everything the board did—or deliberately did not do—was intended to preserve the club, and Haack had no right to undermine the board. After all, was not the Exchange president a mere paid employee of that board? Within the Exchange, the staff began prophesying that Haack would not last ninety days.

However, the board had overlooked what Haack had not: at least two congressional investigations of Wall Street were scheduled for the upcoming year, 1971. To Haack they may well have raised recollections of the Pecora investigations of the 1930s, which resulted in the creation of the first securities laws and the SEC. Haack undoubtedly remembered, too, how another Exchange official, William McChesney Martin, had raised himself to an exalted position in Wall Street by writing a reorganization plan that preserved most of the Street's self-regulatory powers and propelled Martin himself into the presidency. Still today, in the marble halls of the Exchange's sixth floor, many an older Wall Streeter speaks in tones of reverence if Martin's name is mentioned.

The fury the board directed at Haack only gave substance to what most Wall Streeters had accepted as truth for years. Despite the reforms imposed by Congress in the 1930s, the Exchange is still a private club dominated by insiders, floor traders, for example—or crap shooters, as they are sometimes called—and specialists. The tool that enables them to maintain that domination is the Exchange's board of governors, a policy-making body that has ignored the public interest and filled its hours in the years since the Martin reorganization largely with attending to trivia, such as dues payments, and evading major issues of the kind Haack raised. The board has fought hard to avoid developing policies and making decisions on the crucial issues confronting Wall Street. It has provided no leadership,

and even the member firms have complained about its continual preoccupation with outdated problems. As an example,
only the applications for membership, in January, 1971, of
mutual funds too large to be ignored forced the board to act
on the problem of institutional membership, an issue that had
been around for years and one raised in public by Haack.

One such fund, Investors Diversified Services, Inc., of Minneapolis, controlled assets of $8 billion and demanded a seat
on the Exchange for its brokerage subsidiary, Jefferies & Company. Impatient with the board's procrastination, IDS threatened an antitrust suit if the seat were denied. Another mutual
fund, Dreyfus Corporation of New York, also demanded a seat
for its own brokerage subsidiary, Dreyfus Sales Corporation,
but said its demands would be canceled if the Exchange's firms
were permitted to negotiate commission rates.

As happened often before when the Exchange was seriously
threatened and response was unavoidable, the board concocted
a holding action. It hurriedly formed a committee headed by
Lasker himself, which quickly not only approved membership
for mutual funds but approved negotiated rates as well. But
the committee's approval was "in principle" only, and the cries
of protest that issued from board members and the brokerage
firms quickly died when it was realized that the Exchange had
actually committed itself to nothing.

But new crises occurred. In February, 1971, the SEC demanded that the Exchange implement "competitive" rates on
the parts of stock transactions worth more than $500,000.
Arthur Levitt, New York State's controller and trustee of the
state's Common Retirement Fund, demanded either membership or negotiated commissions be granted to reduce the $1.1
million he paid to brokers annually because of the Exchange's
fixed minimum commission rates. Still another big fund manager, Waddell & Reed, formally notified the Exchange that it
wanted membership. This application was followed by one
from the world's largest insurance company, Prudential. Prudential filed its application and also threatened to make stock
trades for others as well as for itself since a number of the Ex-

change's member firms were contemplating entrance into the insurance business.

The board's reaction was a classic case of procrastination. It asked William McChesney Martin to include fund membership in his study. "The question has been studied to death," said Prudential's chairman, Donald S. MacNaughton, who had already steered his company into a membership on the Philadelphia-Baltimore-Washington exchange in the hope of saving $1 million a year in brokers' fees.

Institutional membership and negotiated rates were not the first crucial issues the board has fought to avoid. For years it had avoided dealing with the issue of public ownership of its member firms, although it had permitted many of them to become closely held corporations. Even in 1969, as the firms began to flounder and their partners began clearing out and taking their investments in the firms with them the board resisted giving its approval to public ownership. Permission did not come, in fact, until the board was forced to give it—after Donaldson, Lufkin & Jenrette, whose William Donaldson was himself a board of governors member, threatened to sell stock publicly with or without board approval. Heeding the threat, the board relented, but it is not unfair to say that the board's procrastination over the public sale of stock in its member firms contributed to the downfall of some firms and the loss of thousands—perhaps millions—of dollars by investors whose investments went down with their brokers.

It is easy enough to determine the source of opposition to public ownership. It came from insiders, specialists, floor men, and the managers of firms whose interests coincided with those of the brokerage industry. All of them feared the outside control that public ownership might bring. Yet any real control by outsiders was a phantom fear. The deck was well stacked against it. In the fall of 1969 the board wrote a series of rules governing public ownership of its member firms that insured that the Exchange would remain a closed club—providing the Department of Justice didn't invoke the antitrust laws.

The rules, which were incorporated into the Exchange's

constitution, were written to make any publicly held member corporations, their officers, and their employees answerable not to shareholders, as in other corporations, but to the Exchange itself. For example, at least 51 percent of the shares issued in a member corporation have to be owned by members themselves, allied members, employee stockholders, or employee benefit plans such as pensions. All of these individuals, groups, and organizations are under the direct control of the Exchange, which can censure, fine, expel, fire, or threaten the standing of any of them for even the most picayune violation of Exchange rules. To head off independent buyers of large blocks of member-firm shares, Exchange rules state that anyone owning 5 percent or more of the voting stock in a Wall Street corporation must be either a member or an allied member of the Exchange. Membership, of course, requires board approval. Outside directors are allowed, a generous concession by the board of governors, but a majority of the directors have to be members of the Exchange. Further, any outside director who is not a member has to be classified an "approved person" by the Exchange's governors. As for management, every top executive likewise has to be either a member or an allied member of the Exchange.

As it turned out, the board had little to fear. The Donaldson, Lufkin & Jenrette offering went over like a lead balloon, and few other firms dared to try a public distribution. Donaldson was one of the most efficiently run firms on the Street, dealing only in highly profitable institutional business, and if its shares were unattractive, it was felt that the public would be even less responsive to the stock offerings of less successful firms.

In their quest for sorely needed capital, at least two firms made alliances with rich customers. F. I. duPont, a company that, as we have seen, nearly went under before merging with Glore Forgan & Company, accepted further lifesaving capital infusions from H. Ross Perot, a Texan who controlled Electronic Data Systems. At about the time Perot moved into duPont, a very old and very lucrative firm, Drexel, Harriman,

Ripley, accepted $6 million from Firestone Tire & Rubber. The financial arrangement was made not to save the brokerage from foundering but to expand its business. Besides giving its name to the firm, which became Drexel Firestone, Inc., Firestone Tire & Rubber received the right to buy up to a 25 percent interest—exactly the maximum equity the Exchange permits anyone outside the securities business to hold in a member firm.

Little was said in the Exchange about the new problem facing the board, however. For when duPont and Drexel accepted outside cash—and control—they violated the rule of the Exchange that states that the major business of an outsider buying into a member firm has to be securities transactions. As it has done with so many other problems, the board shelved this one, too.

To be sure, there have been times when the Exchange's board of governors has not had to be forced into action and has acted swiftly and surely during its Thursday afternoon meetings in the Exchange's board of governors room. But this speedy action nearly always has occurred when the board has been dealing with trivia and routine administration related to the time when the Exchange was a private club and its responsibilities were far less onerous. To some observers of the meetings it seems almost as though the board takes refuge in such duties, using them to create a patricians' bureaucracy behind which to hide—at a time when many of its prestigious members are approaching insolvency.

In fact, the board has occupied itself many times with ridiculously trivial tasks, as in the spring of 1970 when it determined that a fee to register member-firm securities salesmen with the Exchange should be raised from $35 to $50. On other occasions the board has felt that only it could decide whether a radio paging system should be installed on the trading floor. The board also has consistently determined holiday schedules not only for the trading floor but for the Exchange staff that often has very little to do with trading.

It was not long ago that the board personally interviewed

proposed members, interrogating their sponsors as well. It even questioned men and women proposed as *allied* members —people who are merely associated with a member firm in some high-ranking capacity and have no real say in Exchange affairs. There is no rule requiring the board to interrogate prospective allied members as they do members. But the act demonstrates how jealously the board guards the pettiest of its prerogatives. Only recently, when it became plain that there was not enough time at a weekly afternoon meeting to attend to such details, did the board finally stop interrogating allied members.

The prerogatives of the board were developed over a period of some 150 years. Until 1817, or 25 years after the formation of the New York Stock Exchange, there was no board of governors. In that year there were only eight firms and nineteen independent brokers. The Exchange's list of securities totaled twenty-five issues. As a securities trading center, in fact, Wall Street was insignificant beside the Philadelphia exchange, which had developed a formal organization as early as 1790. But despite their small size the New York firms and brokers decided to reorganize along formal lines, modeling their administration after the exchange in Philadelphia. The name New York Stock and Exchange Board was adopted; a constitution was drawn; rules were established; officers were elected; and a room at 40 Wall Street was rented to provide space for trading.

At first the administration of the Exchange was a light task. The chief duty of the president, for example, was to call out the names of stocks being traded during the 11:30 A.M. to 1:00 P.M. trading hours. But trading grew rapidly, and by 1856 two vice-presidents were doing the calling. As membership grew, the Exchange's president became more of an administrative head.

When the Exchange first formally organized, there was only a handful of brokers; even by 1835 there were only 75 members. But by 1869 there were 1,060 seats and thousands of applicants seeking membership. It was during that period that the Exchange became an exclusive club. Though there was no formal interrogation by a board of governors, an Exchange seat was considered the personal property of the member, and one could be bought only from a retiring member. The effect was to make the Exchange a truly ingrown group, maintained under the control of aging, rich men with rigid ideas about who should be given the privilege of membership. Even the addition of 40 seats in 1879 did little to alleviate the pressure for membership.

In those years—and until the 1930s—the Exchange was governed by a committee system adopted just after the Civil War. There was a committee to control admissions, another to control the floor, and another to collect money for the family of a member who died. The administration of the Exchange was in the hands of a governing committee of twenty-eight members who had executive, legislative, and judicial powers not unlike the powers of today's board—with one important difference: in those days the governing committee answered to no one; its interests were solely those of its members. Today, because of the reforms of the 1930s (inadequate though they have proved to be), the board must consider the wishes of the SEC, especially in matters that affect the trading public.

Under the administrations of its governing boards of yesteryear and its board of governors today, the Exchange has maintained a high level of *technical* efficiency. Today, for example, it plans to install ultrahigh speed electronic tickers and computers to regulate the trading process. But the Exchange's administrations have consistently avoided the real *issues*. The Exchange tolerated the manipulators of the nineteenth century, then the trusts of the early twentieth century. In the 1920s and the 1930s its administrations knew of the thefts, fraud, and other transgressions in Wall Street, but they did nothing. Even when federal investigations uncovered the extent of the crimes, the Exchange defied the new laws as though it had sovereign powers. For example, it was not until Richard Whitney, the Exchange's own president and head of the governing committee, was exposed in 1938 as a man who had been dipping into the accounts of his customers that the Exchange membership finally consented to accept the reforms of the Securities Exchange Acts of 1933 and 1934. Besides requiring the elimination of a long list of fraudulent trading practices (such as the wash sale and certain short sales) the new laws also called for a reorganization of administration, specifically the hiring of a paid president as the chief executive of a professional staff. Thus the governing committee became the board of governors.

Today's board is composed of thirty-three members, twenty-nine of whom are elected by the membership. They serve for three years, and their terms of office are staggered so that approximately one-third are elected annually in May. Two of the twenty-nine elected as governors are elected to one-year terms as chairman and vice-chairman. The posts are the most powerful and prestigious positions in Wall Street, indeed in worldwide finance. Of the four governors not elected by the members, three are chosen by the elected board from among men outside the securities industry as representatives of the public. The fourth governor is the Exchange president, who is hired by the board.

Since the introduction of the board of governors in the 1930s, the Exchange has asserted over and over again that its board by and large represents the public interest. However it is basically an arithmetic argument. It suggests that because fifteen of its twenty-nine elected governors must be associated with firms dealing with the public, the public is therefore represented by a majority interest on the board. And, the board argues, since only fourteen governors are members whose principal business is conducted on the floor of the Exchange, those governors are therefore a minority, with only minority power.

The assertion is nonsensical for a number of reasons. The public interest is not the primary consideration in board deliberations unless there is fear of intervention by the SEC or by Congress. The board's agendas and its decisions reflect

Article II, Section I of the Exchange's constitution, which states that the governors must regulate and promote only the "welfare, objects, and purposes of the Exchange," that is, the membership. To imply that the public interest is represented because a majority of elected governors do a brokerage business with the public is to ignore a basic characteristic of the club. Men working together in the Wall Street "community" develop associations with each other far more binding than any association developed with a customer. That is why Merrill Lynch, a champion of the small investor in public, has rarely opposed Exchange policy seriously in private.

For many years it was hoped—and the Exchange never did anything to suggest otherwise—that the three "public" governors of the board would be strong exponents of the public interest. After all, they were designated as such—representatives of the public—when their positions were conceived in the reform of the 1930s. The truth is that the public governors have done little—least of all to protect the investing public. Nowhere is there any evidence that they have initiated substantial changes of benefit to the public or have even thought about the public. In fact, their presence might well have been detrimental to the small investor.

The three public representatives have invariably been high-ranking business executives, removed socially and economically from most investors. In 1969 and 1970, for example, the three representatives of the public serving on the Exchange's board of governors were George B. Munroe, president of Phelps Dodge Corporation; Cornelius W. Owens, president of the New York Telephone Company; and Roger Hull, chairman of the Mutual Life Insurance Company of New York.

Few people outside the board of governors know why particular public representatives are chosen. But there can be no doubt that investors have nothing to do with the selection. The usual kind of public representative, given a high degree of integrity, cannot possibly act for investors in an advocate way. First, many of the public representatives head companies that are tacitly indebted to the Exchange for listing their stocks and providing a marketplace for trade. Furthermore, without the cooperation of the Exchange, is would be difficult for them to bring out and place additional issues of their company's securities. Some of the other governors, the very men with whom the representatives of the public meet, may head firms that will be asked to underwrite future issues of stock for the companies headed by the public representatives.

Besides this conflict of interest, there is strong evidence that the representatives of the public do not know what the Exchange's business is all about. Their puzzlement was expressed by high-ranking executive Jack I. Strauss, chairman of R. H. Macy at the time he served on the Exchange's board of governors. Strauss admitted being puzzled from the first. "An outsider with no securities industry connections to take part in their deliberations, I had no firsthand knowledge of the Exchange's day-to-day operations," he said candidly. "I had the usual experience of personal investments in securities, but I had no knowledge of the procedures devoted to maintaining an open market. (This ignorance, it might be pointed out, did not prevent Strauss from accepting the invitation to represent the public interest.) Strauss's naivete was so extensive that in 1965, when the now defunct firm of Ira Haupt took its securities customers down with it, Strauss was greatly impressed by the Exchange's willingness to provide $9.5 million to pay off Haupt's customers. He regarded it as altruism, saying, "The scandal originated outside the securities industry." He clearly did not understand that the firm thought nothing of intermingling the assets of its customers with its own assets and made no provision to protect its customers by, for example, setting aside reserves. Nor did he question the Exchange's failure to do more than provide compensation for the victims. Compensation is simply the penalty Exchange members assess themselves when one of their members is caught doing what they all do. Yet Strauss understood none of this—and, consequently, said nothing about it.

Still, the lack of professional knowledge about the securities industry among "public" governors is not the most important reason for the domination of the board by the insiders. Far more important is the quality of leadership provided by the chairman. The chairman of the board of governors is Wall Street's whip; he is the one who petitions the president of the United States for political and economic help when the club is in danger. It is dubious, however, that the chairman of the Exchange's board of governors has ever had the interest of the investing public foremost in his mind when conducting Exchange business.

Until 1965 the chairman was chosen from among members who operated on the Exchange floor—the specialists or floor brokers who dealt for themselves. These members never caught sight of investors, much less thought about their interests. Only in 1965, as the result of strong pressure from the SEC, did the board agree to alternate the chairman's post between members who conducted retail business and those whose activities were restricted to the floor. Typically, the terms of the agreement with the SEC were evaded by the way in which the Exchange implemented them. Invariably, the man picked from the retail sector is in good standing with the specialists, the floor traders, and others whose interests center on the Exchange trading floor. He usually has a minimum of contact with the public, whose interests, albeit, still retain the traditional low-level of priority.

The first man to emerge as chairman under the 1965 agreement was Gustave L. Levy. Levy had accumulated his Wall Street experience in a retail office, but his firm, Goldman, Sachs, was one of the Street's leading underwriters, a broker-dealer for institutional investors with little or no contact with the average man. For two years prior to becoming chairman Levy had been a hand-picked vice-chairman under Walter N. Frank. Frank himself was a member of Marcus & Company—a specialist firm.

Bernard J. Lasker, a floor trader and the choice of Levy,

followed Levy into the chairmanship. Lasker, too, was a specialist and a partner in the specialist firm of Lasker, Stone & Stern. A staunch member of the club, he had started out in Wall Street forty-two years before as a runner. His partner, Edward Stern, was commonly regarded as "king of the floor traders." With this background, it was unlikely that Lasker would choose, when his term of office expired, a man from the retail offices with a very deep interest in the public. His 1971 successor filled Lasker's requirements admirably. Ralph D. DeNunzio was a securities salesman who dealt with the public for only four years back in the 1950s. Moreover, his company, Kidder, Peabody, is basically an underwriter and corporate finance specialist. Its brokerage is conducted predominantly with institutions. DeNunzio's vice-chairman, Stephen M. Peck, is a specialist who has been a floor official since 1962. His firm, Weiss, Peck & Greer, is also a specialist firm with some general brokerage business.

Lasker was chairman of the Exchange during one of Wall Street's most revealing periods—mid-1969 to mid-1971. One of the greatest bull markets of all time ended just as he became chairman, and in the bear market that followed, the drop in Street income revealed shabby management practices, incompetent office operations, outright stealing of customers' securities, and the shaky financial standings of the firms. Perhaps most incriminating was the inability—or, more precisely, the disinclination—of the Exchange to regulate its own industry.

That disinclination reflected Lasker's overall approach to solving Wall Street's problems. His utterances mirrored an attitude of Wall Street, right or wrong. His solution for Wall Street's problems was higher rates because, as he told an interviewer, the brokerage community requires more revenues—not less—to avoid "the brink of disaster. It's obvious the major firms," he said in May, 1970, "can't go on losing the amounts we know they're losing, forever. If this continues for a prolonged period of time, we could see some problems, and it may be that we would need additional help." Not once did Lasker suggest that major reform was needed—indeed, crucial—in Wall Street. The "help" he was referring to was the U.S. Treasury.

Imperious and impatient, Lasker thought nothing of dipping into the U.S. Treasury to save Wall Street's firms, for he was a classic example of the powerful Wall Streeter. A personal friend for ten years of President Nixon, he led a militant contingent of Wall Streeters to the White House in April, 1970, to demand aid: or else the economy itself, he said outright, would be hurt. Never had there been so overwhelming a reason for stripping Wall Street of its self-regulatory power. But as a piece of blackmail the information served the Street well. No president or Congress would have dared to overturn the Exchange in 1970, for what Lasker said was true. Hundreds of thousands of stock owners in the United States would have lost so much that during a time of recession the resulting economic turmoil would have been inestimable and catastrophic in effect.

Within the Exchange it was felt that the move by Lasker was a beautifully executed power play in the best tradition of the 200-year-old institution. As it turned out, the feelings were proved right. No one in the administration, the SEC, or the Justice Department made a move to interfere with the horrible mess the Exchange's board of governors had helped to create. Once again Wall Street went untouched.

Lasker undoubtedly relied on his personal relationship with Nixon, whose own power base was Wall Street before he became president. Nixon's law offices were only a few steps from the Exchange, and on a sunny day he could occasionally be seen strolling down Broad Street with some of the Street's executives. Nixon's campaign for the presidency was planned to a great degree in Wall Street, and much of the money that was spent in the campaign was raised there. The president's warm feelings for Lasker are unmistakable. When Lasker became chairman, Nixon sent him this telegram: "Dear Bunny: As I mentioned yesterday, I am highly pleased that you have been chosen to head the New York Stock Exchange. Your abilities and qualities of leadership make you exactly the right man taking the job at the right time. Pat joins me in sending our congratulations and affectionate regards. Richard Nixon."

As a *New York Times* writer once pointed out, Lasker's "abilities and qualities of leadership" were vitally important, but in whose interest these qualities would be directed neither the writer nor Lasker spelled out. There is not much question, however, that Lasker's entire approach was to defend the club, and his technique was a variety of holding actions. In the spring of 1970, for example, when Lasker was defending the fixed minimum commission rates imposed by the Exchange, he said that "abolishing them would lead to destructive competition in the industry. The existence of the Exchange itself could be jeopardized." By January, 1971, when the demands of institutions for membership could no longer be ignored, he hurriedly formed a six-man committee and recommended that rates on big block trades be negotiated.

The maneuverings by Lasker and the board were, of course, nothing more than the usual defensive tactics of delay. They were followed, after inside discussion with members, with the SEC, and with others in government, by agreement to accept partial change or reform. The board reacts only to extreme pressure such as the kind that institutions, with their enormous riches and influence, are able to exert.

The commission rates imposed by the Exchange are far more burdensome for the individual investor than for institutions. While individuals pay a $15 surcharge, as much as 50 percent of the normal commissions, institutions get discounts on 1,000-or-more-share-transactions and can negotiate payments to brokers. But institutions had the muscle to achieve what they wanted. By the time Lasker had formed his committee, 20 percent of all trading in Exchange-listed stocks and 35 to 45 percent of all large block trades were taking place away from the Exchange.

Perhaps the only solution to the problem is to strip the board of governors of the regulatory power it now has, even to abolish that power by law. There is far too much at stake to do anything less. Though the stock market may be an index of the economy's health, it is also a major influence in determining that health. An industry so thoroughly interwoven into the fabric of the economy cannot be left in the hands of people so ingrown in their loyalties and so incapable of thinking beyond tomorrow.

11

Presidents

R<small>OBERT</small> William Haack, the fourth paid president of the New York Stock Exchange, came to Wall Street in September, 1967, as a second-stringer. He had been chosen only after the Exchange had been snubbed first, by Edwin D. Etherington, a former president of the American Stock Exchange, and next, almost at the contract signing, by Donald Cook, president of American Electric Power and a former chairman of the SEC.

From the day Haack stepped into the Exchange as its president, the circumstances under which the job went to him produced denigrating comments. "Haack is a hack," went the gossip at lunchtime bar gatherings. Even compliments were of the lefthanded variety since praise of Haack's abilities nearly always was prefaced by higher praise for G. Keith Funston, Haack's predecessor. Funston had made everyone rich, it was implied, while Haack was a mere technician who could not possibly match Funston's performance. Haack had been raised in the industry, and he lacked Funston's inspired, tub-thumping sales abilities.

It didn't matter to the critics that from the beginning Haack had been included among the ten serious candidates in what had come to be called the "Funston Derby." More significantly, Haack's qualifications were unusually fitted to the job at hand, and in many minds, especially at Merrill Lynch and at the SEC, he was a good first choice. Besides having a sensitive feel for the public interest, Haack had special skills, those especially appropriate for coping with the industry's internal problems— the breakdown of its back offices and the growing number of insolvencies among the Exchange's member firms. He was a securities industry professional, something Funston refused ever to become, and he had made a specialty of administration as an executive and industry figure.

The only interruption to Haack's career in the securities business, in fact, had come during a three-year tour of duty in the Pacific with the navy during World War II. After being graduated with a Bachelor of Arts degree in 1938 from Hope College in Holland, Michigan, Haack went to Harvard and earned a Master of Business Administration degree on a scholarship granted by the Harvard Business School alumni in his home town, Milwaukee. During college he took a job as a lathe operator to help support himself (he left when threatened by members of the United Auto Workers union for not joining up). Haack also supported himself earning his MBA by waiting on tables in Harvard's Millin Hall.

Returning to Milwaukee after being graduated from Harvard in 1940, Haack joined the research department of the Wisconsin Company, which later became a securities investment firm, Robert W. Baird & Company. At various times Haack was the firm's syndicate manager and its institutional sales manager. By 1950 he was a partner, a vice-president, and a member of the executive committee in charge of Baird's overall administration.

Ambitious beyond the opportunities his firm could offer,

Haack began accepting a series of posts in the industry that furthered his experience in dealing with its problems. He became a well known figure in Washington and on Wall Street. In 1959 he became a committeeman for the National Association of Securities Dealers (NASD), the organization that regulates the over-the-counter market, and he began lobbying for its interests in Washington. In 1961 Haack was elected to the NASD's board of governors; in 1963 he became chairman of its National Business Conduct Committee. By 1964 he was chairman of NASD, and then, just a few months after taking the job, he became its first full-time paid president.

When Haack arrived in Wall Street, feelings about him were thoroughly mixed. The well managed, well financed firms—the Merrill Lynches—were dismayed by the corruption and incompetence of the Street. They hoped for an able administrator to help to turn the Exchange into a responsible industry leader tuned in to the public interest as well as its own. In contrast, for hundreds of other firms the mere loss of Funston's tub-thumping made Haack seem the lesser of the two men.

For the first three years Haack pleased almost no one. Clearly in awe of some of the Wall Streeters he served and well aware of the diverse interests of its most powerful people, he became the mediator of Wall Street's problems. Moreover, despite the assured manner he displayed in his work and his convincing demeanor on speaker's platforms, he acquired a reputation as a plodder. It was a reputation not entirely deserved. Haack knew very well the character of the Street. Under his predecessor it had grown, cancerously, to 5,000 firms or more run by thousands of men grown arrogant and overly powerful from the money they had made. Most of them simply operated from one day to the next, planning nothing. When their back offices literally stopped and the bear market reduced revenues to recession levels, they were incapable of developing effective solutions. Hundreds of their firms simply dissolved. When they were threatened by institutions seeking Exchange membership, their only thought was to keep the interlopers out. "My job," Haack remarked at one point, "is to move these people into the twenty-first century." But before he dared to try to move them into the twentieth, much less the twenty-first century, Haack needed to overhaul the Exchange administration and build an organization that was efficient and responsive to his authority.

Keith Funston had run the Exchange personally, almost in the manner of a medieval king. The departments were not unlike fiefdoms, occasionally at war among themselves, rarely in communication with one another, and nearly always involved in campaigns to curry the king's favor.

None, however, could ever hope to become so favored as the Research and Statistics Department and the Public Relations and Advertising Department. Both were controlled by the vice-president of public relations and market development and were key elements in Funston's use of the Exchange as a vehicle for selling stocks. Research developed upbeat, one-sided studies intended to lure Americans into the stock market, and Public Relations and Advertising promoted the results of the studies. Year after year the Exchange's researchers gathered statistics showing such "favorable" developments as stock splits, purchases of stocks by institutions (implying it would be wise to follow their leads), and rises in dividend rates.

There were, of course, no studies made of institutions making poor choices or of dividends being cut since unfavorable reports encourage investors to pull out of the market. Even in the worst years the Exchange researchers could find a silver lining in the stock market cloud and could develop statistics showing how sliding stock prices boosted yields. For example, if a $20 stock was paying $1 in dividends for a yield of 5 percent, the Exchange optimistically pointed out that when the stock fell to $10, the yield would become 10 percent.

One of the most effective stock promotions ever made under Funston was the Exchange's Monthly Investment Plan. People could theoretically put as little as $40 a month into stocks on an installment plan. As a promotion the Exchange's MIP was an enormously successful means of getting people into brokers' offices. From there investors were steered not into the MIP but into mutual funds, which paid brokers more (some legitimately and some under the table), or into larger stock purchases, which eliminated the fuss of the MIP's monthly installments. Few brokers wanted to be bothered with the paper work that accompanies so small an investment as $40 a month.

The men directing the Research Department and the Public Relations and Advertising Department inevitably became favorites in the Funston administration, and a promotional pitch rarely appeared in print without a picture of a smiling, confident Funston. In contrast, under Haack these departments languished; key personnel ultimately resigned or were fired.

One case featured Jonathan Brown. Back in 1952 Funston plucked Brown out of a $9,000 a year job with the Sprague Electric Company and put him in charge of research at the Exchange. Funston increased Brown's salary to $14,000 and asked him, as Brown relates it, to "write me a memo of what's wrong with the industry." At the time, trading was bumping along at two million shares a day.

"It was a magnum opus," Brown recalls, "but the gist was the industry wasn't selling stocks and needed a good poke in the ass."

The first result of Brown's report was a marketing study of share ownership to discover who bought stocks, why they bought them, the income of stock buyers, their sex, age, and other data that could be used in a hard sell campaign. Next, Funston hired a public relations consultant to develop a public relations program, and he vastly increased the public relations staff.

Funston brought in Ruddick C. Lawrence to head public relations. Like Funston, Lawrence had major roots in education. Funston had been president of Trinity College before coming to the Exchange. Rudd Lawrence, though not related to the Lawrences of Sarah Lawrence College, had been chairman of the college's board.

Though they performed well for Funston, Brown and Lawrence failed to impress Haack. When Haack arrived, Brown no longer was involved in research. He had become director of public relations for institutional investors, reporting to Lawrence. Then, when the Exchange created its Block Automation System (BAS) to get institutions back into trading on the Exchange, Brown was put in charge of selling the clearly inferior system.

A tribute to Brown's talent is the fact that he succeeded in persuading nearly two hundred institutions and investment management firms to subscribe to BAS and brought $2 million into the Exchange. Yet despite his heroics, Brown received little recognition. Intensely loyal to the Exchange, he was also outspokenly loyal to former president Funston. The promotion to vice-president he so badly wanted never came, and by the spring of 1970, he decided to resign in favor of selling stocks in Bridgeport, Connecticut, for Eastman, Dillon. Brown's farewell party, which was held in the board of governors room, was attended by Funston, who left his new duties as board chairman of the Olin Corporation and his office in Greenwich, Connecticut, to attend. As for Haack, though his office was just down the hall, he appeared only briefly and made no statement.

The departure of Lawrence, who reported directly to Haack, came about much more abruptly. Less than a year after he arrived Haack fired Lawrence for reasons that were never fully disclosed. Some said it was a case of personal dislike. But if that were true, it was also clear that Haack was consciously undermining the enormous prestige of the post Lawrence had held for 15 years as the differences between Lawrence and his successor clearly indicate. Lawrence had had the ear of Funston and had become, therefore, a major influence in Wall Street. In contrast, the man Haack hired, Eugene Miller, knew little about finance. He was not in the mainstream of management in the McGraw-Hill Publishing Company when tapped for the Exchange job, and at the Exchange he reported not to the president but to Haack's executive vice-president, R. John Cunningham.

The farewell party for Lawrence, who joined the staff of

Continental Oil in a position similar to the one he filled at the Exchange, was held in a sixtieth floor dining room of the Chase Manhattan Bank building a block or two from the Exchange. It was a sentimental affair attended by seventy-five or eighty Exchange employees, though no senior staff executive other than those in Lawrence's own department were visible.

Though other firings and departures occurred naturally as Haack overhauled the Exchange administration, it was Lawrence's department that had given the Exchange its style. Consequently, it was his departure that signaled the end of the Funston era. Other Haack hirings and firings gave an indication of his priorities. A vice-president in charge of the Exchange's electronic data processing, Robert B. Grant, was dismissed not long after Haack arrived; the $3.5 million program he had initiated was junked. Then, a year after this, Haack fired John Bermingham, the man he had chosen to succeed Grant.

It is an indication of Exchange morale that the firing created no feelings of sympathy. The Exchange's electronic data processing equipment and programming was, like the rest of Wall Street's, an unfathomable mess, and most staffers felt that firings were justified. Too, interdepartmental charges for using the computers were enormous, in some cases three times the amount outside firms would charge for the same services. Indeed, the Exchange's computers and the ignorance of the low-paid electronic data processing staff were the main reasons why the Exchange's first attempts to establish a Central Certificate Service of stocks failed.

The Haack firings were only the superficial signs of the real upheaval that was taking place, for Haack was committed to adopting the rigid management techniques of most U.S. corporations. When he arrived he said, "Funston had seventeen balls in the air. I propose to decentralize." Not long after he said that, basic change began. He delegated the authority of his own office, distributing precisely worded job descriptions of top and middle management duties and reestablishing a pecking order leading to the president. Over the groans of older, less flexible executives, he introduced formal long-range planning, thereby pinpointing authority and responsibility in exact places. He charged the Exchange's executive committee, which was composed of a handful of his highest ranking vice-presidents and chaired by R. John Cunningham, the hard-running executive vice-president he had brought in from the Midwest Stock Exchange in January, 1968, with overseeing the senior staff planning. The executive committee reviewed the planning of the department executives, including budgeting; they also assumed the job of educating men who had no basic understanding of the role of planning or its mechanics.

In order to keep the pressure on, Haack required those charged with planning—directors, vice-presidents, and men of equivalent rank—to set monthly goals that would lead progressively toward completion of the established plans or would explain why goals weren't being met. Haack also brought in men who were clearly professional managers. Cunningham, for example, had worked at the Midwest Stock Exchange. He had been a management consultant previous to that, and when he left the Exchange in March, 1971, he returned to management consulting rather than to finance. In selecting a replacement for Ruddick Lawrence, an executive with five departments directly responsible to him (advertising, investors information, public information–press relations, special services, and institutional investors public relations), Haack undoubtedly was swayed by Eugene Miller's adherence to the principles and practices of managing as they are tediously denoted by the American Management Association (AMA). Miller knew practically nothing about the securities industry. Yet his lack of knowledge clearly was no handicap in Haack's eyes since he saw in Miller a professional manager of the caliber he wished to have throughout the Exchange.

Miller administered his five departments with a rigid adherence to AMA-prescribed practices. He established a new pecking order, and he picked the brains of his subordinates for ideas. And, as forecast by William D. Horgan, a thirty-year man who attended the farewell party for Lawrence, he made the Exchange a gloomy place to work. "I want tigers," Miller said once. Obviously concluding that Horgan was not a tiger, Miller forced him into an early retirement. Though Haack was forced to veto two major Miller-inspired advertising campaigns, one with *Business Week* and the other with the *Wall Street Journal,* Haack nevertheless remained an enthusiastic supporter of professional management. Thus the man he chose to succeed Cunningham as executive vice-president, Richard B. Howland, was of a similar mold. Before joining the Exchange, Howland had been a management member of American Express.

The formality that Haack introduced to the Exchange did not mean that he was inaccessible, though that often seemed to be the case. Not infrequently a request made in the morning for a meeting resulted in an appointment with Haack the same afternoon. When he met this way with a staffer, knowing that the chain of command had been violated, Haack was informal and friendly without being patronizing. He responded to questions with replies of substance. As might be expected, he invariably insisted that the staffer's superior should be told of the meeting and how Haack had responded.

Still, in general Haack kept his distance from the gatherings of his staff, and consequently few personal relationships developed. Only rarely did he eat lunch in the senior staff room, where discussions were more social than professional, and only occasionally did he appear at parties. When he did so, his stays were short, and thus he frustrated the attempts of men who had hoped to buttonhole him. Even the Monday morning meeting of the senior staff, a give-and-take session that, under Funston was an established ritual, was left to languish by Haack.

Haack's divorcing himself from directly running the Exchange inevitably produced problems. For a start, a communications gap developed between the Exchange management and its members. Not fully understanding Haack's position on issues and not always being able to reach him, the Exchange membership. This occurred a number of times during the staff sometimes distributed contradictory information to the period when the Exchange was proposing higher minimum commission rates to the SEC, and it caused members to complain that they were not being properly informed.

Still, by establishing an administration that ran the Exchange without much personal direction from him, Haack allowed himself time to carry out one of the prime duties of an Exchange president: lobbying.

The duty was also traditional. At least one president before Haack, Emil Schram, had been chosen as a result of his associations with Washington legislators and administration regulators. A former head of the Reconstruction Finance Corporation, Schram had succeeded William McChesney Martin in 1941, as one senior Exchange executive recalls, "to keep Washington off our backs." Schram succeeded admirably. Despite the intrusion of SEC regulation, power remained with the specialists and floor traders of the Exchange, and not once did the cloud of antitrust investigations materialize, Shortly after Haack arrived, the Exchange's Jonathan Brown said, "If Haack is able to do an Emil Schram job on the Washington bureaucrats, especially from an antitrust view, by suave, low pressure personal leadership, he'll end up being a hero."

There was no doubt when Haack was hired that he possessed Schram's capability for keeping Washington at bay. As president of NASD, Haack had moved into a home in Potomac, Maryland, a small community ten miles northwest of Washington. Potomac was a strategic location for a lobbyist, and Haack buttonholed congressmen, SEC regulators, and the Washington press. He became a member of the exclusive Burning Tree Club, the University Club of Washington, D.C., and the Congressional Country Club. One of his constant golfing buddies was Manny Cohen, the SEC chairman during Haack's tenure as NASD president and a supporter of Haack's candidacy for president of the New York Stock Exchange.

When Haack was elected president, he kept his home in Potomac, Maryland, confessing to a subordinate once that he enjoyed it so much there that he preferred to live the life of a commuter rather than move to New York. It was plain from the start of his term in 1967 that Haack's proximity to Washington would be an advantage for the Exchange, for the problems besetting the Street were already emerging. From the beginning Haack was a frequent visitor to Washington, and by 1970 his absences from the Exchange were so extended and numerous that many of the Exchange staff complained to each other about the lack of leadership. Again and again Haack was called on to testify before hearings of both Congress and the administration. In 1968 he was a witness in opposition to tax reform when Congress was considering changes in capital gains holding periods. He was a constant witness at SEC hearings in 1969 and 1970 when the Exchange was asking for substantially higher minimum commission rates. He also testified frequently before administration cabinet hearings and was a White House visitor.

Those appearances, of course, were public ones. Not made public, however, were a series of secret meetings Haack initiated early in 1970 with key senators to fend off investigation of the insolvencies of a number of the Exchange's member firms. For months Haack left the Exchange early on Friday or even on Thursday, not bothering to counter the belief of many of the staff that he was merely leaving the office early for a long weekend.

Regardless of the grumbling heard in the Exchange, it was clearly to Haack's credit that Washington's legislators failed to make serious inquiries into the Exchange's problems even though there was plainly reason to do so, if only in response to the volume of congressional mail from investors critical of Wall Street's bilking and deception. To counter such pressure was not easy, Haack told a meeting of the members in August, 1970. (It was the first time most of them had heard of the campaign.) Haack himself admitted to being physically tired from the effort. It had been a long, sustained rearguard action but one worth the result. There was now no danger from Congress, he assured the meeting. Haack's words proved to be true. There was no investigation of Wall Street until Senator Harrison Williams, of the Senate Banking Committee, announced in the spring of 1971 that he would initiate one—without any thought of recrimination.

In August, 1970, however, Haack's audience gave him not a single sign of praise. Indeed praise was not expected. Haack's tendency to make sympathetic statements about investors, his determination to make over the industry, and his allying himself with the hated and feared Merrill Lynch did not sit well with the more ingrown members of the Exchange. A few months after his report of defusing Congress, the rumblings grew perceptively stronger when Haack suggested in a public speech that negotiated rates on big block trades ought to be given a chance to work. Harold Rousselot, a partner in F. I. duPont, Glore Forgan & Company, criticized Haack for "conducting himself in this manner." Clifford Michel, a partner in Loeb, Rhoades & Company, said he needed a drink before blurting out the words, "It's ridiculous!" Leon Kendall, outgoing president of the Association of Stock Exchange Firms, a former special assistant of G. Keith Funston and a man thought to be pressing for Haack's job, said, "This is no way to handle reforms."

Haack's statements and sympathies, however, were not the only circumstances that invited criticism and opposition. In the place most Wall Streeters saw him, the speaker's stand, he was a cool, self-assured leader who gave his reports from carefully prepared notes. His straightforward delivery, while implying full control over the events he was discussing, did not invite applause or demonstration. He was the organization man, but to Wall Streeters unfamiliar with what this quality meant to the Exchange, Haack seemed aloof and inflexible. In petty fits of temper, people in the Street often recalled Haack's reluctance as an executive of NASD to participate in a fun-and-games session during an Investment Bankers Association convention in Florida.

For all his reserve, Haack still sparked feelings of loyalty, especially from members of the press, whom he cultivated personally. During his years in Washington he had considered Eileen Shanahan, a perceptive reporter for the *New York*

Times, friendly to him and his causes. When Haack became president of the Exchange and Wall Street's shenanigans began to unfold, he was personally hurt when Shanahan wrote articles that were unfavorable to the Exchange. In fact, within the Exchange, for a time, Shanahan became identified as one of the "enemy," a group of press people considered unfriendly not so much to Wall Street as to Haack and his plans for the Street.

Haack felt betrayed, too, in 1968, when he invited the New York financial press to an extraordinarily lavish luncheon. During the meal Haack made some off-the-record comments about how the small investor eventually was going to have to pay his own way in Wall Street. Not realizing that the statement was off the record, Bob Metz, a financial columnist of the *New York Times,* reported the statement in his column the next day, even to detailing the menu. As a result, Metz joined the ranks of the "enemy" and was not invited to the next luncheon. (By Christmas, 1970, Haack had finally cooled off, and Metz was once again invited. He was even given a framed, autographed menu.)

Haack felt betrayed still another time by Richard Ney, the actor turned California broker who in 1970 wrote *The Wall Street Jungle.* In his book, Ney attacked the specialists of the American and the New York stock exchanges, using as a base a 1962 SEC Special Study. Ney had succeeded in getting Haack to grant him an interview, much to Haack's regret. At a meeting of allied members following the book's publication, Haack bitterly referred to Ney as "that bit actor," saying that Ney had lied about the purpose of the book in making his request for an interview. The Exchange considered a suit against Ney, but its lawyers feared that facts that might emerge from the suit would be far more damaging to the Exchange than anything Ney had stated in his book.

Still, even the most prejudiced observer of Haack would have to admit that the extent of his anger was routine when compared to that of his predecessor, Keith Funston. Furthermore, though certain elements in Wall Street wanted to see

Haack ousted, their reasons could be said to stem from the inability of any Exchange president to please the hundreds, even thousands, of diverse interests represented by the Exchange. There is no question but that Haack generates reactions that are far different from those stirred up by Funston, whose legendary anger was incurred by anyone who crossed him—members, Exchange executive, or newspaperman.

Funston, who arrived at the Exchange in 1952 after seven years as president of Trinity College, was the choice of Sidney Weinberg, a Wall Street kingmaker since the days of the Depression. And from the beginning, Funston clashed with the Irish and Jewish mafia, the two factions on the floor of the Exchange that dominate it even today. Funston arrived ignorant of securities trading. He had been an assistant to the chairman of the War Production Board before going to Trinity, and he made it clear that he had no intention of learning the techniques or the jargon of trading.

The breach of etiquette inspired two reactions: some held that Funston was not capable of learning; others maintained that he had no need to since he had, after all, been brought into the Exchange to engineer a hard sell program. In any case, Funston, *the* archetypical WASP, was a natural target of derision and resentment for the members on the floor. Many had been raised in poor circumstances; they were uncouth and largely uneducated. It made no difference to many of them that Funston made them rich by luring millions of Americans into the stock market. He was simply not "their" man.

Of course, the enmity of such opponents affected Funston very little; many others on the floor were staunch allies. Many of the floor traders made fortunes because of Funston, and during his tenure he did not interfere in their administration of the club. So they were not about to destroy a good thing— especially one who, because of his success, was as strong as Funston. In fact, in order to get his way, Funston threatened the Exchange's board of governors with his resignation many times without fear of its acceptance—a gesture that Haack, being in a different political position in the Street, has not and will not make. Only once in his fifteen years as Exchange president was Funston overruled by the board of governors, and that was over a question concerning the listing of Royal Dutch Shell securities. He was not hurt politically.

Funston could threaten the board and ignore some of the floor's most powerful factions with impunity for one simple reason. In Wall Street, where the only real power bases develop as the result of some enormous feat of salesmanship, Funston turned out to be *the* salesman of all time. It was he who, by deft use of Stock Exchange research, public relations, advertising, and his own smiling countenance, persuaded millions of Americans to "buy a share in American business," an Exchange slogan that disappeared swiftly when Haack became president.

"He [Funston] was never accepted by many floor people," says an Irish Catholic associate of Funston, "because he was an academician. He was a Phi Beta Kappa and saw business in an objective way. He was never a part of the securities business. He was Mister Shareowner. His Yankeeism was one of the reasons he was disliked by the floor, which was populated with so many Irish Catholics and Jews. Wall Street operates much like the garment center, and there are similarities that are ethnic as well as other. These are the people this Yankee had to contend with. He was an intellectual snob and could prove it. He had been president of a college, and they didn't like that on the floor of the Exchange. These people were one great big bowl of Jell-o."

This line of reasoning made Funston angry not only with his staff but with people outside, especially critics. Funston spared no one within the Exchange or outside it. He was the martinet, and he did not hesitate to dress down a man, even a favorite, in front of his associates. Members of the Exchange staff often referred to the Exchange, under Funston, as "The Kremlin."

Even a powerful Exchange member was not immune to the

Funston wrath. Harold Bache, the venerable head of Bache & Company, asked his vice-president for public relations and advertising, Henry Gellerman, to assess the attitude of the press toward Wall Street. The assessment, a confidential memo that Gellerman delivered personally to Bache, was not complimentary to the Street. Gellerman said among other things that the press did not believe statements issued by the Street, especially those issuing from the Exchange. Bache made copies of the memo for a confidential internal distribution, but somehow a copy fell into the hands of Funston, who summoned both Bache and Gellerman to the Exchange for a meeting that for Gellerman—Bache has since died—left unpleasant memories. Funston gave both men a tongue-lashing, and Gellerman, very conscious of being a Jew in what he felt was a WASP-controlled Exchange, literally shudders when he tells of the meeting. Funston's anger was so great that Gellerman admits to being actually frightened.

The issue was not whether Gellerman was right in his estimate, though he undoubtedly was. Gellerman had headed Bache's public relations effort for years. He had been with the Associated Press before that, and he knew hundreds of reporters and writers. The issue was *betrayal.* The charge was that Gellerman and Bache had betrayed Wall Street, more specifically, they had undermined Funston's public relations and sales efforts.

That Funston truly believed that one internal memo could destroy the Exchange's credibility is hard to believe. Though he tripled the public relations staff of the Exchange, he himself never courted the press—as Robert Haack would do after him. Further, though Funston's staff turned out thousands of optimistic facts, the majority of them were useless trivia such as a compilation of the number of companies that raised dividends the previous year or the fifty most active stocks during a given period. Almost every release was designed simply to lure the innocent and uninformed investor into the stock market by conjuring up illusions of riches. Most reporters obtained very little substantial information from the Exchange, and they came to rely on leaks for concrete facts. Funston was well aware of this.

It might well have been that Funston, deceived by the frequency with which his photograph appeared in newspapers, especially those out of town, truly believed the press was on the side of Wall Street. After all, demands for reform by the press, when there were any, were written in a wrist-slapping tone. Certainly, this belief in the affinity of the news media with the Street accounted for the shocking displays of anger that occurred when Funston and the Exchange were attacked seriously by the *New York Times,* which had traditionally supported its sister establishment, the New York Stock Exchange.

In the mid-1960s the *Times* began a systematic attack on the way in which the Exchange conducted itself. Funston was outraged to such an extent that he met several times with the publishers of the paper. His approach was one of asserting power, not of pleading for equal time. He brought Walter Frank, chairman of the Exchange at the time, to one of the meetings. To another he brought Frank's successor, Gustave Levy, hoping to put a stop to the editorials. "I have no recollection of any unpleasantness," recalls John B. Oakes, the editor of the *Times* editorial page (the actual writer was M. J. Rossant), though Oakes admits Funston charged him with "irresponsible treatment" in connection with at least one editorial. "I guess we must have driven him up the wall. He cited a lot of statistics once when we were talking about volume discounts at one of the lunches. We also had discounted the possibility of the Exchange moving, as it had threatened, and we had called it a club."

There is evidence that the editorials were part of a campaign to force Funston to resign. The campaign, which included John L. Loeb, one of the Street's reigning elders, as a prime mover, though Loeb will not comment on this, was initiated after the Ira Haupt firm failed in 1965. Coincidentally

tools of the :
ments. If the
senior staff, ev
age investor, t
when many i
greed, incomp
plight origina
stole the stock
clients' accou
ceived custom
brokers realize
them from h
and began tu:
said nothing.

In fact, the
discussed, eve
room, where t
minds were su
their houses, :
streets. Indee
senior staff wh
investors were
these men pro
welcome the a
said in the ne
were so many
that most indi
For some, esp
lockout was n
sell their shar
dent in charg
remarked non
I could walk
find a buyer.'

Perhaps in
integrity, the
special favor

or not, it was about this time that the *Times* editorials peaked in intensity and frequency.

In any case, there are many in Wall Street today who maintain that Funston was conspiratorily ousted. "It was a strong movement," recalls one man. "The group involved felt he wasn't representing the Exchange well. They were upset over a number of things, including the Ira Haupt failure. They didn't like the Exchange putting up all that money. They also saw the handwriting on the wall. There would be more failures. Funston couldn't handle what was coming. The movement didn't come from the floor, either. They were actually split. It came from the highest ranks of the firms, beginning around 1965. Funston quit in 1967."

staffer who is not yet in the top forty but beginning his climb might easily receive a salary of $25,000 (or as much as $30,000) in addition to a Christmas bonus equal to five or seven weeks salary. He undoubtedly would be given the privilege of eating lunch in the senior staff dining room, though he might not be permitted to eat lunch in the Exchange's Luncheon Club on the eighth floor unless he were a favorite. (Permission to eat in the Luncheon Club is granted only by the Exchange's executive vice-president.) How well the staffer ingratiates himself with the Exchange's high-ranking vice-presidents, including the executive vice-president, also determines whether he will be invited to attend the weekly senior staff meetings. As the staffer makes his way upward, three or four promotions will raise his earnings to $75,000 or $80,000 a year.

High salaries and bonuses are only part of the incentive of the senior staffer to remain a loyal tool. While he is emasculated, as one critic sees it, the Exchange extends an ego-feeding power few people exercise outside government. Consider the Member Firms Department and the vice-president in charge, Robert M. Bishop, a thin-lipped, humorless man. Bishop was brought to the Exchange by Keith Funston from Trinity College, where Bishop had worked in public relations. When Funston left, Bishop stayed on even though he had lost his patron. Although Bishop was passed over by Haack when Haack was looking for someone to head the Exchange's biggest division, Operations, which included Bishop's own department, as manager of the Member Firms Department, Bishop is a man with great power. Member Firms is a watchdog agency, a kind of secret police force that investigates the industry. The department even controls hiring among member firms to the extent that it chooses the employment agencies with which the member firms may deal. It can withhold, suspend, or withdraw approval of employment for someone already working in a firm or for a prospective employee. It determines also the income a firm may pay an employee. Even so internal a matter as a salesman's leave of absence is in the province of Member Firms authority.

The department's power among the members themselves is just as extensive. It can force them to appear to testify and to produce incriminating books and papers. It examines the financial questionnaires submitted by the firms to the Exchange and has the power to grant or refuse time to firms to solve financial problems. (In fact, it gave the firms so much time to solve problems of maintaining levels of capital that it undoubtedly contributed to the rash of insolvencies that ultimately occurred.)

For all the powers Member Firms wields, its investigations do not always lead to justice. Securities salesmen are censured every day for violating Exchange rules and securities laws, yet most escape with fines or are given a few days' suspension. If charged under common law for taking funds from a customer's account, for example, they would most likely lose their freedom. The member firms are likely to get off lightly, too. Under the Exchange's exercise of its regulatory function, some firms are more equal than others. The exchange went to great lengths, even to putting up its own money, to save Hayden, Stone but was content to watch the less significant Devonshire Corporation sink into oblivion, taking its customers' accounts with it, though a court action forced the Exchange to reimburse Devonshire's luckless customers. No such pressure was needed on the Exchange, however, in the case of McDonnell & Company, a firm that actually raided the box of securities it held for customers. The Exchange paid out $8.4 million to the firm's 19,000 customers without a murmur of dissent. It was McDonnell's raid on its box of securities, and undoubtedly the raids of other firms, that finally stirred Member Firms on September 3, 1969, to recommend to the board of governors that all firms be required to account for customers' securities by "physical examination" along with a comparison of books and records. Member Firms also called for inspection of brokers by independent accounting firms, but only once a year—thus there would be more than ample time for a firm to use a customer's securities for its own purposes, especially since the department's recommendations did *not* include a surprise audit.

Another truly powerful department of the Exchange, one that wields unusual control over corporations, is called Stock List, headed for decades by Phillip L. West, a genial vice-president who retired in 1971, and now run by voluble accountant and vice-president Merle S. Wick. Stock List receives and processes the applications of corporations desiring to list stocks for trading on the Exchange. Since listing shares for trading has an uplifting effect on a corporation's ability to raise money and to persuade investors to buy its shares, Stock List is in a position to make demands on its corporate applicants. Over the years, in what has been an arm-twisting process, since Stock List can also suspend and remove listings, West persuaded U.S. corporations to tell more and more about themselves. He even was successful in persuading European corporations, who are extremely secretive, to tell more than they are accustomed to—though one company, whose name he refuses to disclose in telling the story, physically ejected him when he became too insistent.

It is assumed that the more corporations tell about themselves, the more investors will be protected. Unfortunately, the increased information West's policies squeezed out of corporations filling out Exchange listing applications (documents that resemble a prospectus in form and content and even require a prospectus in the case of original listings.) does *not* benefit the average investor. True, the information eventually filters down to the "little man," but Exchange applications for listing are not readily available. Even if they were, the average man might be unable to understand them, so full of legal jargon and nonsense are they. In fact, the real beneficiaries of Stock List's efforts are Wall Street brokers and large customers—the institutions—who receive information first. By the time the individual investor has the facts, it is usually too late.

Few other departments in the Exchange offer the men who

run them the kind of power wielded by Member Firms and Stock List, but nearly all the rest have been endowed with status and, in the case of one or two, the opportunity to mold public opinion and to duel with legislators and the Administration in Washington. One department, the Floor Department, can censure, fine, and deny members access to the trading floor of the Exchange for infractions of the rules. It can also examine and reexamine the qualifications and competence of members operating on the floor. Its powers also permit it to approve the registrations of members who are specialists, odd-lot dealers, and registered traders.

As might be expected, little real power can be exercised against the specialists and the floor traders since they represent the most powerful members of the "club" itself. To be sure, a new and relatively powerless member might be cited, but the Floor Department staff steps lightly. At times, it will put the spotlight on a trading rule infraction, but not because it has seen something detrimental to the investor. Usually, the department acts only when the matter in question violates the rules of the club, that is, it offends the other traders.

Perhaps because the Floor Department does step lightly, it is extremely sensitive to criticism, especially any that originates outside the Exchange. For example, Richard Ney's well-documented *Wall Street Jungle* roundly criticized practices among specialists and others on the floors of the American and the New York exchanges. This thoroughly enraged J. William O'Reilly, vice-president of the Floor Department, who for weeks after the book's appearance inveighed against Ney to all who would listen, especially during lunch in the senior staff dining room.

The Exchange's molder of public opinion is called Public Relations and Investors Services, a misnomer if there ever was one. The department floods the land with press releases, seemingly informative. Most, however, end up in the waste baskets of editors because of the trivia they contain. The identity of the companies with the greatest numbers of shares outstanding is hardly the kind of information investors need.

This tends merely to publicize the names of companies listed on the New York Stock Exchange. Invariably, the department ignores or answers with bland nonsense truly pertinent questions. For example, an honest question—"Is AT&T stock, which you list and thus implicitly endorse and approve, since it meets your listing standards, a good investment at the price your specialist has arrived at?—is likely to be answered with the response: "See your broker." Never is a specific broker suggested since to do so would anger those not suggested.

One of the major powers of the Public Relations and Investors Services is to supervise the advertising and public relations of member firms. It reviews and approves *before publication* all advertisements and other communications and can fine, censure, and suspend employees who violate Exchange standards of "truthfulness" and "good taste." The chore is not a routine one since many of the member firms' advertising ideas originate with their principal executives, and the disputes that have developed between the firms and the Exchange at times have been fierce. In 1969, the firm of Edwards & Hanly put on a series of televised ads, one of which included Joe Louis, the retired heavyweight champion. The suggestion was clear that among all the firms, Edwards & Hanly was strongest. It was a suggestion, however, the department saw as being detrimental to the other member firms, and the ads were killed, though not without real resistance from Edwards & Hanly. Edwards & Hanly was not the only firm to question the judgment of Eugene Miller's department. Advertising copy of Dominick & Company, which also suggested it could do more for investors than other brokerages, was also vetoed.

The department that defends the prerogatives and self-interests of the Exchange, such as self-regulation and higher commission rates, is called Civic and Governmental Affairs. It is led by a moody, sometimes peevish vice-president, Donald L. Calvin, a man very much aware that, unlike most others of the senior staff, he answers only to the president.

The fuel for Calvin's battles is developed by another vice-president who answers directly to Haack, William C. Freund.

An economist and academician, Freund has been harnessed by Haack to the Exchange's lobbying chores. He develops forecasts of the economy's direction and of the direction of the market (upward, Freund's projections show, to an average of 23 million shares a day by 1980). Freund was also responsible for the development of thousands of pages of wearying statistics and questionable fact to support the Exchange's bids in the last few years for higher commissions. Freund is, in fact, one of the Exchange's key men, as the vice-presidential status assigned his position shows. Under Funston's leadership, the Exchange economist also reported directly to the president, but the research and statistics staff reported to Public Relations, which used the material to develop publicity. Under Haack, the research and statistics staff reports to Freund.

Not all of the senior staff wield great powers, of course. Many an executive has to make do with mere salary and status. The Exchange's real estate executive, for example, an articulate architect named Tyrell G. Rogers, has had the responsibility in recent years for the design and construction of a new Exchange building, to be built on a landfill at the foot of Wall Street in New York's East River. In 1970, however, Rogers was forced to watch the millions that had been earmarked for the new building evaporate, along with his building plans, as the Exchange used the funds to stem insolvencies and pay off the customers of bankrupt firms.

As though the gags of money, power, and status are not enough, the Exchange also employs a Big Brother technique that keeps all but the most extreme mavericks in line. Basically, the technique threatens key men with the loss of their jobs. The Exchange uses what is called a "key man assessment sheet" to determine who will go and who will stay. The sheet deals in "jeopardy criteria factors" and amounts to an insidious piece of man-watching. In all, thirteen factors are used to assess a key man, after which he is assigned a "criticality rating." His "gripe level" is noted, as is his "commitment." If he doesn't like his job and makes the mistake of saying so, or if he is unclear about his role, or if he even thinks he sees an unfavorable personal future and feels left out, he is in deep trouble. Found guilty of just two or three of these "offenses" his criticality rating becomes one that "bears watching." If he is a friend of someone who has been fired, that, too, is held against him, as is being passed over for promotion. A criticality rating of 4 or 5 on the 13-factor scale puts him in the "serious" category. A rating of 6 or beyond puts a man in a "critical" position.

However, for most of the senior staff of the Exchange there is not much danger of being rated critical or even of being watched. The majority easily qualify for the one favorable rating: "solid." Most of the senior staff are loyal to the point of being argumentative in response to any criticism of the Exchange. The reaction of the Floor Department's O'Reilly to the Ney book, as well as Haack's similarly bitter reaction, is evidence of how the staff accepts criticism from the outside. Most staffers work so hard to please their superiors that they are suspicious of each other and compete intensely to win favor.

One of the more significant displays of jealousy, departmental partisanship, and rivalry among the senior staff occurred during 1969 and 1970 when the Member Firms Department was investigating firms whose financial reports to the Exchange showed they were in violation of capital rules and heading for bankruptcy. Like secret police, the Member Firms staff, which took all its cues from Bishop, kept things secret, thus thoroughly annoying others on the staff who had a right to know, if only generally, what was happening. In fact, it was not until the summer of 1970, when Haack himself revealed the extent of Wall Street's insolvencies at a meeting of allied members—which senior staff were permitted to attend—that personnel in other departments learned how bad things were.

Weeks later the story was repeated with relish, even malice, when it was learned that many a Member Firm investigator had been faced down and shown the door by executives of the firm under investigation. After this had happened a number of times, the Exchange was forced to call on high-ranking executives of other firms to act as investigators. The Member Firm staffers, it was learned, had been deceived again and again with false figures, inflated estimates of a firm's capital, and plain lies about a member's ability to stay afloat financially. Among the top forty of the senior staff, where it was not decorous to do much more, the story was told with a grin or two. At lower echelons it was told with the straightforward attitude that the Member Firms personnel got what they deserved.

In June, 1971, when Bishop himself was transferred laterally to the newly created post of vice-president for special projects, it was felt, with some justification and no little satisfaction, that he had fallen victim to brokers' complaints of his "Heil Hilter attitude." For many of the staff, the failure of Member Firms, which seemed in the mainstream of things more than the other departments, undoubtedly helped deepen a feeling or two of insecurity.

Few of the senior staff give much evidence of brilliance. Few can be regarded as belonging to that ephemeral group of people known as the Establishment. Many, in fact, have worked their way up from low-level jobs, acquiring their positions by functioning as the hard-working drones the Exchange requires. Some are merely professional executives, faceless, of the sort readily found in most U.S. corporations. Many, in the course of advancing their careers, have attached themselves to a powerful individual in the upper reaches of the staff, or to one of the Exchange's ruling class on the trading floor—a specialist or a floor trader.

Eugene Miller, for example, fetched and carried for R. John Cunningham, the executive vice-president of the Exchange, until Cunningham resigned early in 1971. Many a time, after getting a telephone call from Cunningham, Miller would abruptly leave a meeting he himself had called, causing as many as ten or twelve highly paid people to wait while he literally trotted down the hall to Cunningham's office. Professional executive that he was, Miller insisted more than once to his subordinates that instant response to a superior's wishes was an absolute necessity. Interestingly enough, when Cunningham left the Exchange, the staff consensus was that Miller was vulnerable. In fact, rumors circulated constantly that Miller was hunting ·for another job. Miller, however, was promoted to senior vice president.

The story of another vice-president shows how such attachments, really political alliances, can be traumatic. The vice-president in this case was Cecil MacCoy, the man in charge of Special Services until his retirement in June, 1971. Basically, his duties at the Exchange involved supervising the visitors' gallery, publishing the *Exchange* magazine, and organizing receptions for VIPs. Such duties were obviously of fringe importance, well removed from the mainstream, and clearly beneath a man of MacCoy's rank. Yet MacCoy, who admits he spent the last decade "protecting my rear," felt lucky still to be working at the Exchange at the time of his retirement.

In 1952, when Keith Funston arrived, MacCoy was in charge of the Exchange's entire public relations organization. He was also in favor with one of the Exchange's most powerful and demanding men, John A. Coleman, chairman of the board of governors a number of years ago, and broker (a word that understates the relationship) for the Catholic church in New York. "Coleman scared the hell out of everybody when he talked to them," an employee of the Exchange for forty years recollects when asked what made Coleman feared. It was undoubtedly Coleman's friendship that made MacCoy feel somewhat more powerful than he actually was. In any case, shortly after Funston arrived at the Exchange in 1952, MacCoy, a huge, white-haired man whose gruff manner overwhelms some associates, responded to Funston's commands sluggishly or not at all. Jonathan Brown, Funston's head of research and an admitted Funston supporter, says, "He gave Funston snot." No matter what it was MacCoy gave Funston, only the intervention of Coleman saved MacCoy from being ousted. But from then on his responsibilities were undermined severely, step by step, in what was clearly a fall from power directed from above.

Despite the fact that they often make their way due to internal political alliances, MacCoy and others of the senior staff regard themselves as self-made men. The appellation is not necessarily complimentary. For example, many an employee literally trembled in the presence of a burly Exchange controller named Leonard Bedarf who retired in 1970—to the relief of hundreds of employees. MacCoy, too, was a terror to some of his employees. He ordered his staff around in the manner of a sweatshop boss and kept a bottle of Scotch in his desk to ease the pain of an extreme sciatica condition. When the pain became too great even for the whisky to dull, MacCoy roared at his help. His secretaries admitted to losing weight while working for him, and one, despite taking tranquilizers, succumbed to a nervous breakdown.

It may be unfair to suggest that the senior staff, as men, were to blame for what was generally a hard-nosed approach to lower-level employees. The Exchange itself, as a matter of policy, clearly adopted the stance that most "people are lucky to be working here," an attitude that explains the Neanderthal approach in evidence time and again.

Once, for example, a young Jewish boy reported to his job as a page on the trading floor wearing a yarmulke. On the floor, where fashions in clothes are sometimes extreme and in bad taste, the yarmulke seemed so threatening, for reasons not clear, that the boy was given a choice of taking it off or giving up his job. The situation filtered up to Charles Klem, vice-president of administration, who confirmed the decision. By then the story had leaked to the newspapers and took on embarrassing racial tones—when there actually were none. In what was an embarrassing retreat, Klem distributed a memo throughout the Exchange admitting that employees, even the lowest, had the right to wear apparel required by their religious beliefs.

The stern, unremiting standards the Exchange staff requires of lower-level employees turns up in general situations as well as in individual incidents. For years the staff had been successful in holding down membership in the United Financial Employees Local 205 of the Office and Professional Employees International Union. Though most Exchange employees once were content to accept the vicarious thrills of working for the Exchange in lieu of a fair salary, that contentment had disappeared pretty thoroughly by 1968. It was during that bullish year that it became clear that the boom in trading had benefited Exchange employees little in terms of compensation. A membership drive by the union attracted large numbers of employees from every department of the Exchange. The dissatisfaction was also evident in the turnover of employees. In 1968, the turnover was, according to the union's estimates, well over 25 percent. The Exchange's reaction to the unionization was to cut back sharply on merit raises, saying to managers who sought them for subordinates that the union would be winning raises for them. The result of this could have been easily anticipated—and perhaps it was. In 1969, according to the Exchange's own analysis, the turnover rate leaped to 42 percent. In 1970, it settled back to 37 percent. Significantly, the key-man rate of departure was only 7 percent in 1969 and 11 percent in 1970.

The question that might reasonably be asked is how does a management—the senior staff—manage to create such bad relations. The flip answer is that ingrown attitudes come naturally in Wall Street, which is actually a tight little community whose power structure is modeled after the caste system. But there is more to it than that. Many a senior staff man models his outlook on the idea that the Exchange is a kind of fort, which it resembles architecturally. Its high walls and three very narrow entrances can be defended by very few men. In May, 1970, when the Exchange received a series of bomb threats, the simple defensive strategy was to station platoons of guards at all three entrances. For a number of weeks, too, the Exchange turned the visitors' exhibit rooms into a squadroom for New York's police.

The Exchange's senior staff, not surprisingly, is intensely conservative. When riots did erupt in May, 1970, the Exchange was not the target, but among the senior staff the feeling most prevalent was that the police were justified in flailing away at the "hippies" who were "causing trouble." When the police did not flail away and kept order, but the New York Port Authority's construction workers left off building the World Trade Center to do what the police had not done, sympathy in the Exchange favored the hard-hats by a high ratio. Indeed, as the senior staff ate its lunch to the sound of noontime battles eight floors below, the comment generally was that the hippies were getting their just deserts. Inevitably, in conversations the shooting of the Kent State University students came up, and though many a staffer himself had children at college, the comment generally was "they got what they deserved."

That comment was uttered, too, in reference to the individual investor, whose mail documenting the misdeeds of brokers had been arriving at the Exchange in great numbers since early in 1968.

Part 4

The watchdogs—where they fail

13

The SEC

EARLY in 1969, 200 experienced individual investors living in 10 cities of the United States were asked in a Lou Harris poll what they thought of self-regulation in the securities industry. Unhesitatingly, a majority, 60 percent, said it was inadequate. When Harris reported his findings in detail to his client, the American Stock Exchange, it was clear that the word "inadequate" was itself inadequate to describe the high feeling and, in some cases, outrage expressed by the polled investors.

Selected for their sophistication as investors, the 200 ordinarily could have been counted on to endorse stock market operations. Yet they felt there was a strong "need for stricter controls, enforcement, and rulings." There was a need, they said, "for government to police the industry [since] the industry's real interest was only its own gain. Thus, no type of self-regulation would be adequate." The cop needed "to keep the ball game on the up and up," they said, "was a more powerful Securities and Exchange Commission." It was a call for help, but, without greater change, a change in government practices, one that is unlikely to be acted on. The SEC, the only guardian public investors have, generally has failed in the task assigned to it by Congress.

At the American Stock Exchange, and a few months later at the New York Stock Exchange, the sentiments so clearly put by these substantial and usually self-reliant customers—recent victims of Wall Street's back office incompetence and fraud—made hardly a ripple. The poll was talked about at staff meetings, but that was the end of it. Even if the poll's findings had been distributed generally, or for that matter turned over to the SEC, the effect would have been slight. The SEC had no need of a poll to tell it how investors were being man-handled by brokers. Complaints to the SEC had soared from a few thousand to fourteen thousand a year by 1968, and it was estimated that the brokers were themselves getting four hundred thousand or more complaints a year—albeit they ignored most.

An overworked agency ever since it was formed in 1934, the SEC has also been hamstrung in its leadership, if not in its powers. Despite attracting men of integrity to its staff of accountants, securities analysts, and lawyers over the years, the SEC's commissioners and chairmen have looked for culprits not so much among Wall Street's leading hundred firms or within the Exchange but among lesser fry in the industry. Generally, it has cracked down only when there have been obvious and blatant violations, as in the case of Merrill Lynch vice-president, Archangelo Catapano, who transmitted inside sell information about McDonnell Douglas Aircraft stock to more than a dozen mutual funds while small investors were being told to buy. Even when the SEC does take action the penalties are light—the Merrill Lynch vice-president still works for the company. Very few leading Wall Streeters go to jail for their offenses.

The SEC's chairmen almost invariably have been appointed

from among Wall Streeters and political cronies of presidents who have chosen not to be outraged, as were Ulysses S. Grant and George Washington, when Wall Street sought to make allies of them and exploit the power of their office.

Indeed, the very first chairman of the SEC, Joseph P. Kennedy, was exactly the kind of speculator whose activities the securities laws were intended to curb. When he was appointed to the SEC chairmanship on June 30, 1934, by Franklin D. Roosevelt, Kennedy had just been tracked down as a stock pool participant by Ferdinand Pecora, the Congressional investigator whose findings were the basis for the present securities laws. Pecora also was the architect of a law that would have taken away the self-regulatory powers of the Stock Exchange to a great extent, but Kennedy, as SEC chairman, gutted it.

James M. Landis, a lawyer who succeeded Kennedy in 1939 as chairman of the SEC, was not the hand-picked candidate of President Roosevelt that Kennedy had been. But Landis was undoubtedly highly favored by the Stock Exchange, having won favor in 1932 by defending the Exchange against a plan of New York's Mayor Fiorello LaGuardia to regulate it. Landis developed the astonishing argument that to regulate or limit speculation, which is the actual business of the Exchange, was unconstitutional.

Not surprisingly, liaison between Wall Street and the Administration was unusually good during Landis' term of office. As chairman of the SEC, Landis continued to favor Wall Street and successfully aborted attempts by his staff to introduce reforms. If studies critical of the Street were begun, he starved them for funds. If by chance one emerged anyway, it was buried. If its authors became restless over the burial, they were fired.

Landis left the SEC in 1943, but in later years he became a major Washington figure, a favorite of presidents, and an expert on the affairs of the regulatory agencies. To many observers, especially the press, he seemed a sinister figure, lurking in the White House and accumulating power, and for many their suspicions were confirmed in December, 1960, when Landis presented his Report on Regulatory Agencies. On the grounds that the regulatory agencies, the SEC included, were too slow in their adjudicating proceedings and also were neglecting their planning and "creative" functions, Landis recommended that the powers of the agencies be delegated to a White House czar. Since Landis himself was installed in the Executive Office of the White House at the time, many a newspaper writer inferred that Landis was nominating himself.

Within Congress the proposal ran into enormous opposition, for Congress, which had created the agencies, regarded them as quasi-judicial organizations not to be controlled by the White House. Said Senator John McClellan: "Nobody wants them to get under the domination of the president, or the assistant to the president, or somebody else. We want to keep them independent, where they exercise a judgment and a judicial function of their own, influenced by the merits and by the record, and not one that comes under the executive branch of the government."

By April, 1961, President John F. Kennedy had backed away from the Landis proposal in the interest of maintaining good relations with Congress. There was no need, anyway, to confront Congress. Presidential assistants charged with Exchange and SEC matters have always maintained a large degree of control over the SEC if only because SEC chairmen rarely get to see presidents. They ordinarily deal, therefore, with White House assistants who are not above climbing to power on their backs. More than one SEC chairman has had a difficult time determining whether to respond to the requests of a presidential assistant, not knowing whether the president's own wishes were being spelled out. Most chairmen have stepped lightly, though, for the assistants can wield real power. For example, on at least one occasion in very recent times a presidential assistant actually has *chosen* the chairman of the SEC.

The SEC chairman who was chosen was William J. Casey,

and the man who chose him by virtue of being put in charge of the search, was Peter M. Flanigan, a White House assistant to President Nixon. Himself a former vice-president of Dillon, Read, a Wall Street investment banker, Flanigan is one of the Street's very own. He also served in the late 1960s as a political fund raiser in the Street for the Republican Party. Once, Flanigan hosted Wall Streeters at a luncheon to raise campaign funds for Whitney North Seymour, Jr., who twice was elected a New York state senator and in 1970 was appointed as a U.S. Attorney by President Nixon. Inside the White House, Flanigan invariably represented Wall Street's interests, arranging meetings between Exchange chairmen and the President—in the spring of 1970, for example—or plumping hard for Casey, a man the Street raised no objection to as head of the SEC.

Casey had no special background in the securities field. A tax lawyer, he had never displayed much interest in securities except as a means for reaching his self-proclaimed goal of making a lot of money. But he had been a large contributor to Republican campaigns, giving $17,500 in 1968 alone to six different campaign committees.

Casey was also a partner in the New York law firm of Hall, Casey, Dickler & Howey. One of the other partners, Leonard Hall, was for many years chairman of the Republican National Committee. Moreover, in 1960, during Nixon's unsuccessful presidential campaign, Casey had been Nixon's writer of foreign affairs position papers.

Upon his appointment in March, 1971, Casey revealed a policy the script for which might well have been written by the administration of the Stock Exchange. The most urgent problem as he saw it was the creation of a sounder capital base for Wall Street's firms; consequently, though the profits of brokers had "risen rapidly" in the months before he took office, he intended to keep in effect the $15 surcharge on securities trades of 1,000 shares or less. Moreover, Casey said, the SEC needed more data to determine whether the surcharge, levied early in 1970 as a temporary relief to brokers, was still needed. "It would not be prudent to remove it," Casey said, though why he did not explain.

On May 24, 1971, Casey took what he called a "flexible view" toward a proposal of his own staff that Wall Street firms put aside a cash reserve of 100 percent against the unencumbered cash balances that their customers leave with them. Though the use of customers' cash balances is Wall Street's major disgrace since the firms use them as though the money is their own—sometimes even speculating in the commodities market with funds—Casey was not enthusiastic. "I think there's a real question whether 100 percent is needed to do the job," he said. Though he pointed out that Congress had created SIPC, a corporation to insure investors against brokers' insolvencies, he failed to point out that protection was limited to $50,000. Considering Wall Street's record, which Casey did not bring up, a 100 percent reserve seems clearly necessary.

In Casey's early administration, his real concerns seem almost planned to raise fake issues, or at least those not requiring immediate attention, and to direct attention away from Wall Street's more infamous deeds. He is concerned with the different accounting systems corporations use, for example, and thus with the difficulty that arises when one tries to compare one corporation's financial well-being with another's. The problem is a real one, but hardly of a kind that needs top priority now. Casey is also concerned that securities markets of the future provide accurate and complete information on prices and volume and that this be distributed quickly. As he knows, this is one thing Wall Street has done extremely well, the Exchange having poured large amounts of money into it.

The sad truth is that Casey is following the pattern set by the men who came before him. Moreover, whenever the SEC has been led by men who have tried to assert authority, they have been largely unsuccessful. The one or two SEC chairmen who have succeeded have paid a price—a sudden deceleration, for example, of their careers.

There is the case of William L. Cary, chairman of the SEC between 1961 and 1964. When Cary arrived, the stock market was a raging bull, with new issues, that perennial and classic indicator of a market out of control, being sold for huge premiums above the offering prices. Price–earnings ratios were at classic bull market highs, and as usual Wall Street's back offices were failing to deliver securities to each other at an alarmingly high rate. Amidst all this, the roof, so to speak, fell in at the American Stock Exchange where an SEC investigation resulted in the expulsion of the leading specialist firm, Re, Re, & Sagarese.

For the newly arrived Cary, a vigorous administrator, the corruption at the American Stock Exchange was a stroke of luck. An angry Congress demanded the SEC investigate, and with an increased budget, Cary initiated the 1961 Special Study of the Securities Market. Completed in August, 1963, the study was the first major examination of Wall Street since the 1930s, and it provoked the staff of the SEC to conclude that, in the case of the American Stock Exchange, self-regulation had been abused not in single instances of misconduct but in a general deficiency of standards and a fundamental failure of controls.

True, the report found that corruption and incompetence were not quite so bad as in the 1930s but bad enough to stimulate Congress into passing the Securities Acts Amendments of 1964. One part of this legislation required smaller corporations—those that might bring out new stock issues—to disclose as much as large corporations with shares listed on the exchanges. A second part raised the required qualifications of brokers and dealers and placed them under stricter disciplinary controls.

Such legislation, of course, raised Wall Street's hackles along with its standards of honesty. But Cary had ruffled feathers before. From the beginning, he had insisted the Exchange's floor traders be banished, and the infighting that developed over that issue brought Exchange president G. Keith Funston rushing from New York to see President Johnson on March 15, 1964. Only an outcry in the press forced Funston at the last minute to deny that he was visiting the president for any other reason than "to get acquainted," and the affair died when Cary extracted an agreement from the Exchange to reduce the number of floor traders from 300 to 30.

There is no question but that Cary was an effective chairman of the SEC. The American Stock Exchange put in new administrative controls, and in the bear market of 1969 and 1970 there were few days in which the selling reached the kind of panic proportions floor traders often induce by their own short selling. Nevertheless, unbridled new issues trading in the 1968 bull market, the back office boondoggles that occurred, and the financial failures of many firms show strongly that there is still much to be done.

As for Cary himself, though he had seen a new securities law passed, the fight wearied him, and he went back to teaching law at Columbia University. In his book *Politics and the Regulatory Agencies* Cary admits that only one company wanted him as a chief executive officer after he left the SEC. But he was not surprised by the lack of demand for his services among those he had regulated, for he had raised the question of personal independence almost immediately on taking the chairman's job. Cary had approached his SEC job in a unique way: he did not concern himself with being liked, grabbing power, trying to further a career in the administration, or putting in time while waiting for a job in the securities industry. Perhaps that is why one of Cary's staunchest supporters, the *New York Times,* said he was shrugged off.

The man who followed Cary into the chairman's seat at the SEC was Manny Cohen, a lawyer and an SEC commissioner during Cary's tenure. He, too, regarded Wall Street as remiss in many ways: the Street had failed to merge the hundreds of small, inefficient firms; office automation was lagging; and planning was non-existent. But Cohen's style was that of conciliator, and he even volunteered the SEC's services and facilities to help modernize the Street. Unlike Cary, who brusquely criticized self-regulation and, six years after leaving the SEC, questioned the sovereignty of the Exchange, declaring it "has hardly demonstrated a capacity for leadership in the public interest," Cohen raised an image of a helpful SEC. He discussed things in private with the Exchange, whose officials took to calling the meetings "tête-à-têtes."

However, even Cohen's faith in the conciliatory path was shaken to its core when, in 1966, he tried to persuade the Exchange's member firms to disclose their financial affairs. The SEC had been policing the finances of firms operating in the over-the-counter market since 1964 but could not extend this function to include Exchange firms because of their refusal to provide data. Disclosure by the Exchange's member firms would be the "longest step," Cohen said, in finding out how the industry ticks. If the member firms had consented to Cohen's request, the great string of brokerage failures in 1970 might have been avoided. But divulging how they "ticked" was the last thing the member firms wanted to do, Thus, the reply Cohen got to his request was a mixture of bombast and questioning his right to know.

For example, Albert Pratt, a partner in the firm of Paine, Webber, Jackson & Curtis, deplored the idea that the SEC thought it had a right to know about the private finances of a private firm. Said Pratt: "There is a difference between a publicly owned company that has to report to shareholders and a private firm with public responsibilities." The logic might escape the concerned investor, but the statement was consistent with Pratt's view of the SEC, for he also took the agency to task for obstructing, not promoting, the "profitable conduct of our business."

The Investment Company Institute, a lobby and trade association representing the mutual fund industry, wondered to what "meaningful uses" the SEC would put the information.

The American Stock Exchange, only a few years removed from the scandals that had resulted in the Securities Acts

Amendments of 1964, feared, of all things, that self-regulation would be jeopardized.

At NASD, the over-the-counter market's regulating trade association, the then president, Robert W. Haack, insisted that the SEC single out the areas of finance it wanted to look into, then justify its need for specific information.

Needless to say, Cohen was stunned not only by the united front of the opposition but also because he had talked in advance, as usual, with the Exchange leadership and believed that he had reached an agreement. At the Exchange, needless to say, no such agreement was admitted. Its position was that reporting their financial status would increase their member firms' costs, undermine self-regulation, and even weaken competition in the market—though the Exchange did not explain how any of these results would follow a change in regulations.

Cohen left the SEC in 1968. He had not accomplished as much as Cary, but he had been effective—especially in his eventually successful battle against giveups. It was probably with relief that he turned to practicing law in Washington. In any case, so complete was his retreat that Casey, upon seeing him at a meeting of business writers in Washington in May, 1971, said that Cohen, who had been out of office less than two years, looked familiar, but that he could "not place him." For the men who are not mavericks the rewards from being an SEC chairman, or even one of its four commissioners, can be extraordinarily good as we shall see.

Cohen's successor, Hamer Budge, was the sort of chairman who, by walking a narrow line, succeeds in offending no one. At first Budge upset the Exchange's management by refusing to participate in the tête-à-têtes begun by Cohen. But the Exchange's fears that he would be uncooperative proved unfounded. From the beginning Budge seemed torn by the plight of the small investor and by a desire to remove himself, personally, from the center of the storm. When the Exchange, early in 1970, proposed to raise commission rates and burden the small investor with most of the increase, Budge said, "I will not go along with the proposal. I think it is the duty of the SEC to preserve the small trader. I think it would be a real tragedy if the day ever came when a grandfather could not buy shares of AT&T for his grandchild."

Budge also spoke publicly about the number of complaints the SEC was getting from investors. In December, 1969, he told a Florida meeting of the Investment Bankers Association, the élite of Wall Street underwriting, that the SEC was receiving complaints at a rate of fourteen thousand a year. He estimated that brokers were receiving twenty-five to thirty times as many. Securities were being delivered, he said, to investors as much as eighteen months late. Money due investors was being delayed or never sent them. Account errors were going uncorrected, compounding original errors, and customers were finding it impossible to get a simple response or acknowledgment to inquiries.

After stating these facts, Budge said: "The dealer who sells securities to a customer, or the broker who buys securities for a customer, will violate the anti-fraud provisions of the securities laws if he has reason to believe that he will not be able to deliver the securities with reasonable promptness." It is interesting to note, in the context of Budge's remarks, that in 1968, 1969, and 1970 at least fifty Wall Street firms, all of whom were carried on lists at the Exchange restricting them from soliciting business, could have been but rarely were so charged. Among them were Goodbody & Company, Hayden, Stone, F. I. duPont, McDonnell & Company, Blair & Company, Gregory & Sons, Amott, Baker & Company, Meyerson & Company, Fusz-Schmelzle & Company, Kleiner, Bell & Company, Dempsey-Tegeler & Company, and a great many more.

Unfortunately, Budge's hard line in public and his well-known sympathy for the small investor were never really transposed into hard and decisive action during his tenure as SEC chairman. One reason was Budge's age. When he took the job as chairman, he was already sixty-eight years old and admittedly tired. When he resigned, late in 1970, he was nearly seventy. Budge also undermined his effectiveness, especially in the eyes of some congressmen, by the revelation, five months after he became chairman, that he had been considering job offers from Investors Diversified Services, a Minneapolis-based manager of mutual funds. IDS, in fact, is where Budge landed, eventually. But though he left at the peak of a stormy stewardship, it would be wrong to question his sincere desire to change the securities industry's ways. There was just too much to do, and Wall Street wielded too much power—especially in the White House.

While Budge stood behind legislation to force mutual funds to accept a fiduciary responsibility in the manner of banks, initiated a major study of institutional investors, supported the idea of negotiated commissions, and was an early supporter of legislation to insure investors against Wall Street insolvencies, he provoked no enmity in the Street for his stands. IDS, at least, saw no reason not to take him on as an executive. Budge was well intentioned, but he did not really make much trouble—perhaps, for the Exchange, this is the best combination of qualities in an SEC chairman.

It has not been uncommon for the securities industry to reward SEC administrators who do not display vigorous tendencies to regulate. One New York regional director of the SEC, Mahlon Frankhauser, became a vice-president of the New York Stock Exchange and then an executive with CBWL–Hayden, Stone. Neither Frankhauser nor Budge, however, could match the ascent of Ralph Saul, first an analyst for the SEC, then a commissioner. Saul regarded the Stock Exchange and the SEC as partners in regulation and saw no difference in his service to either. In Wall Street, his attitude clearly was regarded as enlightened. As an SEC commissioner in 1962, when William Cary's Special Study disclosed the problems at the American Stock Exchange, Saul was regarded by the specialists as "one of the few people at the SEC who was reasonable." Soon afterward, Saul became president of the Amex.

Saul served in that post until March, 1971, maintaining all the while that "the exchanges are doing the job of self-regulation effectively and in the public interest." Then Saul, who would have been a serious candidate for the job of president of the New York Stock Exchange had Haack been ousted, accepted an offer from the First Boston Corporation, an underwriter. It was a job that Saul himself implied would make him wealthy.

Despite some of its chairmen and commissioners, the SEC has asserted its authority at times in ways not associated with developing special studies or goading Congress into passing legislation. Not entirely coincidentally, one of the more impressive periods of action came when the agency was headless. This was in late 1970 and early 1971, after Hamer Budge had left and before the appointment of Casey had been approved by the Senate.

SEC actions taken in that period were those of the staff, anxious perhaps to establish some gains before a political appointee stifled them. What makes the period significant is that the SEC finally extended its role from looking for crooks and swindlers *outside* the securities industry to looking *within* it. For the first time, the SEC began inspecting the books of brokerage firms closely, including those of the Exchange's member firms. SEC investigators began checking the firms' cash positions and even counting, one by one, stock certificates being held for safekeeping to determine whether the number they actually found agreed with the number on the firms' books. Those firms that refused to cooperate were threatened with court orders. When account books and executives alike disappeared, the investigators merely bided their time until both showed up.

Finally, the SEC staff forced some firms not only to give up financial information but to file *weekly* reports with the SEC showing current assets and liabilities. The unfortunate side of it all was that the SEC, operating as usual in semisecrecy, released no names.

The SEC staff even investigated the New York Stock Exchange. For the first time in half a dozen years, SEC inspectors ran a check to determine whether the Exchange was indeed enforcing its rules for minimum net capital requirements, and they even subpoenaed internal memoranda when the Exchange balked. The contents of Exchange memoranda may, in fact, have led to the transfer of the Exchange's chief investigator and head of its Member Firms department, Robert M. Bishop, to another, less sensitive job.

What the SEC investigators discovered at the member firms and at the Exchange supports arguments for the end of self-regulation in Wall Street. The capital base of many a firm, rather than consisting of solid assets such as Treasury bills and cash, was found to consist for the most part of non-marketable stock. Some firms failed to show liabilities on their books, and a few didn't even know what their capital position was. For many an investor, the new-found zeal of the SEC was welcome.

No one can be sure that these actions of the SEC staff augur well for the future, especially with Casey now installed as chairman. But if Casey does want to go down in history as an important figure, he has all the authority he needs. The Securities Exchange Act of 1934 set up the machinery to regulate the markets and the dealers and brokers operating in them, and it gave the commission far-reaching powers of enforcement. Only the control of credit, which was given to the board of governors of the Federal Reserve system, was denied it.

From the beginning, the SEC was given the right to examine the organization, the financial structure, and the nature of a brokerage firm's business. It has the right to enforce the Act and hand out criminal penalties of fines up to $10,000 and imprisonment for up to two years for individuals. Stock exchanges can be fined up to $500,000. But as the next chapter shows, law enforcement agencies—the SEC included—have been reluctant watchdogs of Wall Street and its clan.

14

Wall Street flouts the law

Iɴ the 1930s a cowboy movie sheriff named Tom Mix rode to fame astride his "wonder horse," Tony. He rounded up crooks, who were often portrayed as a town's financial leaders, and he uttered such words as, "Straight shooters always win; lawbreakers always lose." Inevitably, Tom Mix proved his point in each picture. As the straight shooter and the honest lawman, he always got his lawbreaker.

But Tom Mix, the cowboy sheriff, never had to ply his trade in Wall Street, a community where straight shooters do not abound and lawbreakers have a strange immunity from prosecution.

It might be that some of the immunity exists because modern lawmen and prosecutors find the jargon, the techniques of finance, and the secrecy of Wall Street impenetrable. Indeed, it is not always easy to determine when a Wall Streeter is breaking the law, even when the sleuths know their way round. We have already seen, for example, how the SEC was for years unable to get a look at Wall Street's books because the firms simply refused to show them to anyone, especially to the SEC. Yet all the time the SEC had the requisite authority. It simply refused to assert its authority.

Defiance, however, has been merely a symptom of the real problem of enforcing the law in Wall Street, for as long as there has been a Street, authorities of all kinds—in the exchanges, the regulatory agencies, the local and federal administrations—have shown a profound reluctance to initiate actions. Indeed, Wall Street's history is filled with stories of the failure of officials at all levels to act. Entire legislatures have been bought off, as have mayors, councilmen, judges, and policemen. For example, Cornelius Vanderbilt and Daniel Drew each bribed New York's entire Common Council of Aldermen, including the infamous Boss Tweed, in their fight to control New York City's Harlem Railroad; they bribed the New York State legislature as well. In his fight with Drew, Vanderbilt even bribed a New York judge and got him to issue an injunction against the directors of the Erie Railroad forbidding them to repay a $3.5 million loan to Drew.

On the federal level, Wall Street has had unusual influence with presidents, especially the Republican presidents of the 1920s who undoubtedly administered their office with blinkers on so far as Wall Street was concerned. The excesses of those years, as we have seen, were extreme. Wall Street also had unusual influence with President Roosevelt, who appointed Joseph P. Kennedy, one of the all-time great speculators, to head the SEC, and with President Nixon, who has adopted a blinkers-on attitude reminiscent of the presidents of the 1920s. As a result of its influence at all levels, the Street too often sucessfully has intimidated its opponents, and from this sort of success has grown a feeling among its members that they are immune from the laws that other men must live under. Even when blatant skullduggery has been unearthed and there was no way to avoid a hearing, trial, or other adjudication, the punishments meted out to the guilty have been as ineffectual as no punishments at all.

For example, in December, 1970, the SEC, the New York Stock Exchange, and the American Stock Exchange almost simultaneously charged Kleiner, Bell & Company, a Beverly Hills firm, its president, Bert S. Kleiner (one of Martin Mayer's "new breed on Wall Street"), and a vice-president, Ralph J. Shapiro, with a long list of violations of federal securities laws and Exchange rules. Kleiner, Bell had recommended to investors that they buy the stock of a conglomerate, Commonwealth United Corporation, while all the while the firm itself was selling the stock on the basis of inside information. During 1968 and part of 1969, Commonwealth United stock had risen sharply, but unknown to investors the company was expected to lose $61 million in 1969 alone. (Kleiner once told Mayer, "I'm just trying to make money.")

This particular complaint originated with the American Stock Exchange. But official trouble over Commonwealth United for Kleiner, Bell had come up before. In October, 1969, the SEC charged that a registration statement and proxy material issued by Commonwealth United were false and misleading since they did not disclose the close relationship between Kleiner, Bell and Commonwealth United. The SEC also found that Kleiner, Bell had mixed customers' fully paid for securities with securities it used to secure the firm's debts. In fact, the New York Stock Exchange charged that Kleiner, Bell had improperly "used $889,285 of customer securities for collateral." Further, said the Exchange, Bert Kleiner and Ralph Shapiro had "improperly been reporting restricted securities for inclusion in the firm's capital and that this had assisted the firm in not reporting a violation of capital requirements from January, 1970."

Getting customers to buy while insiders were selling and using customers' securities as collateral for their own debts were only part of the charges. The SEC charged that in 1968 Kleiner, Bell manipulated the price of Omega Equities stock by bidding for it and then purchasing it at increasingly higher prices. All the time Kleiner, Bell was making its sham transactions it was recommending to its customers that they buy Omega shares. It was a very old ploy and one the SEC said violated the antifraud provisions of federal securities laws.

Despite the number and seriousness of the charges, *no one* involved ever came to trial. Kleiner, Bell as a firm and Bert Kleiner and Ralph Shapiro as individuals consented to the findings of the SEC and the exchanges without admitting anything. The penalties they accepted were the revocation of Kleiner, Bell's registration as a broker-dealer and the barring of Kleiner and Shapiro from association with any securities broker–dealer. The exchanges expelled the firm and the two men from membership or from association "in any capacity with any member or member organizations" of the exchanges. As is often the case, Kleiner, Bell stayed in business, not as a brokerage house, but in its investment banking capacity.

As for the individual investors Kleiner, Bell had been telling to buy Commonwealth United and Omega Equities, they took their losses. It may be that the exchanges, the SEC, and law enforcement agencies felt the same way about them as Bert Kleiner did when he said, "They are a new breed of wealthy men, still unused to what they have. They don't have the concept of conserving capital. They've tasted it. They went to Las Vegas and lost $17,000, paid $15,000 to $20,000 for a painting. So they'll put up $50,000. Maybe they'll lose it, but maybe they'll make a million."

The truth is that the customers themselves feel a lot differently. Until the advent in recent years of class action damage suits, which can be initiated by individuals in *everyone's* interest, investors have been relatively helpless, and Wall Street has never been truly taken to task on behalf of individual investors. It was always the outsiders that the guns were aimed at—the corporations issuing stock, the corporate raiders, the common thieves who stole securities, and even employees of Wall Street firms. In August, 1970, however, when the Exchange decided it would not reimburse the customers of three insolvent firms—First Devonshire of Boston, Charles Plohn & Company of New York, and Robinson & Company of Phila-delphia—lawsuits brought by some of the victimized customers reversed the Exchange's view. Indeed, the Exchange itself is a defendant in a $3 billion suit brought by the National Shareholders Association, an organization of small investors formed in July, 1970, that opposes the Exchange's fixed com-mission structure. In a suit brought in Federal District Court in New York, the association said the nation's investors had been damaged to the extent of $500 million by the fixed commissions naming, in addition to the Exchange, the Ameri-can Stock Exchange, the Association of Stock Exchange Firms, and the brokerage houses of Merrill Lynch, Bache & Company, Walston & Company, Paine, Webber, Jackson & Curtis, and F. I. duPont, Glore Forgan & Company.

There have been a few times when Wall Street has done more than slap the wrists of its élite, and investors have not had to do the job that assigned regulators should be doing. But any observer or chronicler of such exceptional periods— which is what they were—would do well to look beneath the surface. Vigorous prosecution has come about almost only when the Street has feared that inaction would result in the loss of a privilege or a prerogative, or worse, result in action by an angry Congress.

Thus in December, 1961, Edward T. McCormick, president of the American Stock Exchange (and a former SEC commis-sioner), was forced to resign by the Amex board of governors following the ouster of Gerard A. Re and Gerard F. Re, a father-and-son specialist team in the firm of Re, Re & Sagarese, who had been found by the SEC to be guilty of manipulation of stock prices and of fraud. McCormick, who had made per-sonal stock transactions through the Res, might still have escaped punishment but for the fact that the SEC had also found that the self-regulatory process had failed abysmally during McCormick's presidency. The two factors were just too much, and a reluctant Amex board was forced to get rid of the embarrassment they were confronted with, especially since Congress had commissioned William T. Cary, the newly arrived chairman of the SEC, to embark on a Special Study that would result in 1964 in amendments to the securities act.

Of course, the classic case that demonstrates Wall Street's willingness to throw its own to the wolves if it feels threatened is that of Richard Whitney, president of the New York Stock Exchange during most of the 1930s. As we have seen, Whitney, who in 1938 was sentenced to a ten-year term in Sing Sing prison for appropriating the securities of customers, was as much a victim as his customers, ending up in prison not so much because he had taken their securities as because he was in the way. He was a leader of the old guard opposed to a faction led by William McChesney Martin that was prepared to introduce administrative reforms demanded by Congress. Whitney had been appropriating his customers' securities since 1926, and his need for funds had been well known in Wall Street since he was a consistent borrower. Two months after he was exposed in 1938, he was in jail. One month later the reforms were passed, for in the aftermath of the scandal, opposition crumbled.

The fact is that Wall Street has never really felt that the appropriation of its customers' securities is a crime. It has always intermingled its own with its customers'. Thus, despite the fact that McDonnell & Company took securities it was holding in safekeeping for customers—actually stole them, forging the necessary signatures—and even accepted payment, as scores of Street firms did in the late 1960s, for securities purchased by customers knowing it would be unable to deliver those securities (another grounds for action), there is *no* public record available to suggest that the house was ever charged. Instead, the penalties levied on the firm and its principals by a paternal Stock Exchange amounted to liquidating the company and using Exchange funds to return money and securities due McDonnell's customers. It was a little like allowing bank robbers, upon their capture, to go free if their parents gave back the money they stole. Tom Mix, of course, never would have held still for such practices.

At the SEC a decision in April, 1970, merely barred McDonnell's chairman, T. Murray McDonnell, from assuming any material or supervisory job with a securities firm without prior SEC approval. Yet that approval is no more than anyone else must get. In another exercise in futility the SEC revoked the license of McDonnell & Company as a broker and dealer in securities. Like Merrill Lynch, the firm consented to the SEC sanctions without prejudice, as did T. Murray McDonnell, who consented to findings that he merely failed to exercise the type of supervision that would have prevented violations of antifraud regulations of the Securities Act. Specifically, he had failed to advise stock buyers of the "true condition" of the firm's fouled up back office, its books, and its records. The SEC said that he also had failed to tell customers of the firm's failure to comply with financial requirements and of "large operating losses" experienced by the firm between September and December of 1968.

There is strong reason to believe that Wall Street breaks the laws on a widespread basis, but modern crime-busters prefer to look the other way. The records may be buried in both the Exchange's and the SEC's files or even in the files of elected prosecutors, but the inferences of widespread abuse are plain enough. They showed up early in 1971, for example, when the SEC began forcing Wall Street firms to file weekly, instead of annual, financial reports. They showed up, too, when the SEC's investigators insisted on personally counting the securities the firms were holding in safekeeping for others, then comparing the count with the figures shown on the books. Hints of wrongdoing were implied when the SEC began requiring brokers for the first time to maintain a capital reserve against money that customers left on deposit with them. Clearly, unless there had been abuses throughout the industry and violations of fiduciary responsibilities, no such measures would have had to be taken. Nor would the Stock Exchange have accepted them.

The new "hard" stance of the SEC simply represents after-the-fact correction of lawbreaking routines. In April, 1971, the SEC decided that Goodbody & Company, a firm married to Merrill Lynch in a shotgun wedding demanded by the Stock Exchange, should not be permitted to keep its license as a broker-dealer. Like McDonnell, Goodbody had not kept its records straight. The penalty, slight though it was, came *after* Goodbody had become a part of Merrill Lynch and, thus, no longer really existed.

The reluctance to prosecute the men and firms at the top in Wall Street is not confined to regulatory bodies such as the Exchange and the SEC. The most serious and famed crime-busters, those elected by the people or appointed by the federal government, show a marked tendency to avoid running down high-level crime in the Street. The late Tom Dewey, for example, was undoubtedly New York's most successful crime-buster. But Tom Dewey pursued what is euphemistically called "organized crime," members of the Mafia and waterfront murderers. New York's very respected district attorney William Hogan has not made his reputation by digging away at Wall Street, although clearly there has been enough reason to begin an investigation. Nor has New York State's respected attorney general, Louis Lefkowitz, initiated actions against any Wall Street principals, although he and his staff consistently develop surveys of wrongdoing. At the Stock Exchange, in fact, Lefkowitz is considered a friend.

Even the U.S. Attorney in New York, Whitney North Seymour, Jr., has seen no reason to look into Wall Street at high managerial levels, although his office on Foley Square is only a few short blocks from the Street. Of more interest to him, apparently, is the run-of-the-mill kind of thief. An inquiry in the summer of 1970, a period when Wall Street's insolvencies were at their peak, showed that the typical wrong-doer being pursued by the U.S. Attorney's office was hardly in the big leagues of crime. In a Tom Mix scenario he might have been one of the thugs working for the crooked banker. The U.S. Attorney's files showed, for example, that for transporting about 7,100 shares of stock between Newark, New Jersey, and New York City in the summer of 1968, two men, Edward J. Farris and Joseph M. Mainer, received the following sentences after being prosecuted vigorously: Mainer was given one year each on three counts of an indictment, or a total of three years to be served concurrently; Farris was sentenced to eighteen months on each of three counts, the sentences also to be served concurrently. A third man, William P. Petracca, who was not captured until March, 1969, was found guilty on two counts and sentenced to concurrent terms of five years on each. The presiding judge, noting that Petracca was very young, placed him on probation with the requirement that he go back to school or go to work.

Whether the sentences seem unduly harsh is not the issue. They may well be typical of sentences most people would receive upon being successfully prosecuted for comparable crimes. The issue is whether the machinations of *all* Wall Streeters should not be approached with equitable treatment in mind. It might even be considered reasonable that when guilt is established in the case of Wall Street principals the penalties ought to be greater, for a greater degree of trust is involved. Brokers are permitted by the Federal Reserve, for example, to borrow the funds of customers, interest-free, to lend to other customers, at high rates of interest. Brokers also may keep the securities of customers in safekeeping, though not without the express consent of those customers and not without segregating the securities from their own. Other laws require brokers if they are privy to inside information to divulge that information on an equitable basis.

Time and again, brokers have ignored the responsibilities that go with such privileges—as in the case of McDonnell & Company, Merrill Lynch, Kleiner, Bell, and a long, long list of others. Indeed, the extent of brokers' failures and the many times they ignore the laws, as shown by the near-daily accounts of SEC investigations, suggest strongly that harsher penalties are needed. The facts also suggest that the Exchange's regulatory practices are sadly deficient. When it was granted the privilege of self-regulation by the Securities Act of 1934, the Exchange agreed, in turn, to make the Act work and to make it work in the public interest. That was its part of the deal. Yet all too often its actions have abrogated that agreement, as a look at the mood of the Justice Department suggests.

In the eyes of the trust busters, the New York Stock Exchange is a lawful monopolist entitled to fix prices and to control 80 percent of the securities market. The basis for this view is the Securities Exchange Act of 1934 and an opinion of the U.S. Supreme Court, which heard an antitrust suit brought against the Exchange. The Court determined that the Act, though not saying so specifically, implied that the Exchange was entitled to some degree of antitrust repeal. The degree of repeal was clearly limited, however. The Court said: "Repeal is to be regarded as implied only if *necessary* to make the Securities Act work, and even then only to the minimum extent necessary."

In the years since it was granted regulatory power, the Exchange frequently has tried to broaden that implied repeal of the antitrust laws to its maximum reach—not necessarily to make the Securities Act work but to benefit its insider members. As a result it has run afoul of the Justice Department, which has often had to point out to the Exchange that it is a public institution, not a private club conducting its affairs only in accordance with the interests of its members.

One recent occurrence came late in 1969 when the Exchange decided that its members needed to sell stock in themselves to the public if they were to survive. There were twenty-two conditions in the proposals the Exchange put before the SEC. Practically all of them were written to limit sharply the control and influence of investors and to permit those already in control to stay in control.

At the Justice Department, which had been asked by the SEC to comment, the proposals were tested against the Supreme Court edict. Were they necessary to achieve some legitimate goal of the Securities Exchange Act of 1934? Or were they designed to keep outsiders out? "The SEC," said the Justice Department in a memo signed by Richard W. McLaren, assistant attorney general, and three other attorneys in the department, "should carefully distinguish between proposals which actually broaden the Stock Exchange membership base and those which only benefit the existing members by permitting them to go public. The former are more likely to meet the requirements of the Exchange Act and the antitrust laws." Late in the memo, the trust busters said that there was "a strong inference that the limitations were primarily designed to exclude institutional investors from membership."

The Exchange maintained, of course, that its proposals fell within the scope of the Exchange's right of self-regulation, and, further, that they were necessary to carry out the purposes of the Securities Act. Then it really fired both barrels. The Exchange counsel, a prestigious lower Manhattan firm, Milbank, Tweed, Hadley & McCloy, asserted that there could be no antitrust liability because the proposals were subject to the SEC's powers of review. As might be expected, the Justice Department denied such a notion. Congress, it said, provided general antitrust exemption only when there was comprehensive economic regulation, including authority over rates, marketing areas, and extent of service as in the transportation industry. The Congress expressly provided antitrust exemption for companies whose actions had the approval of their regulatory agency. The SEC, however, was not charged with comprehensive economic supervision of Wall Street.

Despite its opinions that the Exchange has run the securities industry at times for its members' exclusive benefit, no one can say that the Justice Department has taken the Exchange and Wall Street to task. The Department's dealings with the Exchange are a dialogue—no more—intended to raise little more than an illusion of activity. There can be no question that the Justice Department is basically friendly toward the Street. It has initiated few actions and excuses its lack of activity by saying it does not wish to "intrude" on the SEC.

The Department of Justice did nothing, for example, when Merrill Lynch acquired Goodbody & Company, when the Exchange forced a whole string of mergers in 1970, and when the Street's odd-lot firms, already reduced to two, merged into one in 1970, thereby eliminating all competition. In contrast, the Justice Department has been vigorous in its pursuit of antitrust violations among U.S. corporations, so vigorous in fact that its chief, Richard McLaren, was attacked by a former chief, Lee Loevingers, for breaking up corporate mergers that did not restrain competition at all but in McLaren's view merely had the "potential" to do so. As a result of the Department's less-than-vigorous law enforcement in Wall Street, antitrust actions there invariably stem from civil suits filed by shareowners or by firms that have been blocked by the Exchange from doing business.

A few years ago a number of shareholders in the Lehman Corporation and other mutual funds brought a class action suit against the Exchange and four member firms. The suit asked treble damages, charging that the Exchange and the firms had engaged in a coercive conspiracy, fixing minimum uniform rates of brokerage commissions and applying those rates in violation of the Sherman Antitrust Act. Since the Securities Act of 1934 did not expressly grant immunity from the antitrust laws, the suing shareholders claimed the Exchange had no immunity. The courts admitted that though there was no express exemption, a repeal of the antitrust laws, as determined by the Supreme Court, did exist. The mutual fund shareholders left the New York District Court after being told that the antitrust laws were inapplicable.

In recent years, however, there has been reason to believe the Exchange and its member firms are not as immune to antitrust laws as they have always thought they were. The issue now is restraint of trade, and the plaintiffs—though not in court—are a group of Wall Street firms doing business independent of the Exchange: Weeden & Company, which makes markets in Exchange-listed stocks; the First Boston Corporation, a large underwriter; and M. A. Schapiro & Company, a firm that was for years an independent dealer in bank stocks.

As far back as 1964 the M. A. Schapiro firm charged that an Exchange rule (number 394) prohibiting members from trading with non-members in stocks listed on the Exchange was in restraint of trade. By forcing member firms to deal only with each other, the Exchange assured that most trading in a stock would remain within its own preserves, that is, the floor of the Stock Exchange and the specialists stationed there. Once an issue was listed, member firms could not trade in it except with other members. In the case of Schapiro, the rule was more than disadvantageous—it was disastrous. A major market maker in bank stocks for years, the firm became a direct victim of the Exchange's rule when bank after bank was listed on the Exchange in the late 1960s.

Whether it was the case of Schapiro or the combined complaints of other firms operating in the so-called third market —Weeden, First Boston, and a host of lesser lights—the Justice Department early in 1971 called for the abolition of rule 394. This move strikes at the heart of the private club for it clearly suggests that the Exchange has been in restraint of trade. By the spring of the year, the Exchange was close to striking down the rule. With rule 394 gone, member firms would be free to deal with just about anyone—and a membership on the Exchange would carry far less value. Indeed, much of the Exchange's power would disappear.

For investors, the results of the abolition of rule 394 could be extraordinarily advantageous. Though member firms are required under Exchange rules to buy or sell stocks at the best price, the best price has not always been that found at the Exchange. Indeed, the third market only grew because it could make a better deal for its customers—generally institutions. The third market's growth is, perhaps, the strongest indicator that the Exchange has become a fat, immovable monopoly in which competition has largely disappeared, as indicated by the lack of competitive prices for stocks. If this is so, then immunization from antitrust laws no longer shields an institution theoretically acting in the public interest but in actuality acting first in its members' interests. Not only should the laws of antitrust be applied to the institution itself, but the common law should be applied to the members and principals of the Street as well—and vigorously. Then, we would see changes.

15

Wall Street and the press

I honestly didn't start out as a critic of Wall Street or the Stock Exchange. But as a reporter and editor I covered the Street for fifteen years, and in those years it became clear that criticism was needed. Major things hit me. There was the nineteenth century atmosphere at the Exchange. There was the enmity of the Wasp, Jewish, and Catholic elements on the floor. There's no place for this in the twentieth century.

"Another thing that struck me were the ethical standards. They were improving, but generally they were inexcusable. There was more than one standard. They *did* believe in insider information. The whole Ted McCormick thing at the American Stock Exchange in the 1960s showed that. He was in on the deals, yet he was a former SEC commissioner.

"But the ethics were bad all over. Even I was offered deals to keep still. Free rides. Stock. A chance to get in without any money. The offers came from both firms and individuals."

The comments above are those of Murray J. Rossant, who for a number of years in the 1960s was an editorial writer for the *New York Times* and one of the most implacable foes of corruption in Wall Street known among newspapermen. A reporter for *Time* as a young man, Rossant went to *Business Week* magazine in 1953 and became its finance and stock market editor. It was there that Rossant blew the first whistle on Ted McCormick, the convivial president of the American Stock Exchange, with an article that began: "Something is rotten in the state of the American Stock Exchange." Rossant joined the *Times* editorial board in 1962, from which post he attacked the New York Stock Exchange as well as the Amex. When he left in 1967, he became director of the 20th Century Fund, a New York philanthropic and research organization with a stock portfolio then worth $25 million.

Besides adding *New York Times* stock to the Fund's portfolio, Rossant continued to put Wall Street under a microscope by financing economic and investment studies.

If the outrage of G. Keith Funston was any measure, Rossant was one of the more effective and unflagging enemies of corruption and incompetence in Wall Street. More than once after Rossant had written an editorial disclosing an unsavory practice in the Street, the Exchange buzzed with stories of how Funston, in luncheon meetings with the *Times'* publishers, had demanded that the editorials end and even that Rossant, and his boss, the *Times* editorial page editor, John B. Oakes, be fired. Oakes denies the stories but admits, "I can certainly recall some perfectly clear differences of view."

There was good reason, of course, for Funston's angry reactions. Rossant saw the Exchange, as ruled by Funston, as "a good nineteenth century organization," and he admits that he "made Funston's life miserable." Rossant even suspects that the *Times* editorials he wrote "paved the way for Funston's departure," which he insists was an "ouster" engineered by Wall Streeters themselves: "He was really a figurehead for the crapshooters on the floor, a front man, though an extraordinarily good public relations man and a drummer."

In Rossant's opinion, however, Funston never cared to learn the gritty details of the securities business, nor would he come to grips with its internal problems. Then, when the back office problems began to develop and when the institutions began trading in other markets to avoid the Exchange's high commissions, a faction that included Merrill Lynch and other powerful firms began looking around for someone who understood the mechanics of trading and could cope with the emerging problems of the industry. In the fall of 1967, Robert Haack, an industry professional who might have written his own job description, was hired as president.

Rossant wrote no editorials defaming Funston, personally. On the contrary, he raised issues, especially when he saw the extent of Wall Street's greed. Back in 1958, for example, when Rossant was with *Business Week* as its markets editor, the Exchange attempted to raise commission rates. After conversations with some of the Street's executives, Rossant wrote that a rise in the rates was far from needed.

A few years later at the *Times*, he wondered in print why the very small investor, the odd-lot buyer, should pay an additional fraction of a point over the price that a round lot buyer pays. "Why should trading in odd-lots," he asked, "be any more costly than other transactions now that automation is here?"

The same question, of course, might well have been asked in the late 1960s and early 1970s in reference to round lot buyers of 1,000 shares or less. While institutions were getting discounts on trades greater than 1,000 shares and paying little, or in some cases nothing, but that part of a trade worth more than $500,000, the buyer of a few hundred shares was paying the Exchange's high fixed commission rates *plus* the additional $15 surcharge levied in 1970—"temporarily."

Once, Rossant also told his readers that the cost to the investor of a stock trade relative to the value of the stock was higher in the United States, despite the enormous volume, than in Europe. The cost in Europe of a stock trade involving $1,000 was 1 percent on the average. In Switzerland the cost relative to the value was a very low .25 percent. Rossant calculated that the cost in New York was 1.75 percent. The significance of the figures, of course, was that despite vastly greater trading volume in the United States, volume that would lend itself to cost-cutting automation, there clearly had been no economies passed on to the investor. Rossant's charge was verified in 1970 when the Exchange proposed raising its minimum rates again. With volume reaching twenty million shares a day the Exchange admitted that the proposed new rates would skyrocket the cost of a transaction to 2 percent of its value, on the average.

Stock price manipulation and fraud also came under attack from the Rossant typewriter. In April, 1963, the Special Study of the SEC revealed widespread abuses in both areas. To Rossant the puzzle was why the findings were turned over to the perpetrators themselves to act on. In a *Times* editorial he said: "No matter how conscientiously Wall Street cleans house, the dishonest and the unscrupulous will thrive as long as they can prey on the gullible and the greedy."

He said, further: "The need to protect the public demands elimination of every last vestige of the day when Wall Street was a closed shop of professional investors and speculators. There can be no dispute with reforms that safeguard the interests of the public. The financial community cannot maintain privileges without responsibility." Though written in 1963, the words are as appropriate now as they were then. Indeed, they may be more so. For the alliance of institutions and Wall Street firms in the market today could well create a "closed shop of professional investors and speculators" to the disadvantage of the investing public.

When Rossant left the *Times,* the deep concern he had shown left with him. The men who followed him on the editorial page had a more academic bent and were less inclined to engage the Street in righteous warfare. Leonard S. Silk, the current financial writer for example, is a voluble, pleasant economist who took over Rossant's chair in 1970. An editor in the Economics Department at *Business Week* when Rossant was markets editor, Silk had worked for the Brookings Institution before going to the *Times*. A man not inclined toward initiating reform, his editorials, especially those concerning Wall Street, have much less sting than the Rossant variety even though the need for critical appraisal of the Street has been far greater than during the Rossant days.

Not that criticism has died. A *Times* Washington reporter, Eileen Shanahan, though lacking the open-end an editorial page provides for critical observation, has been writing articles for years that reflect concern for the public interest and the prerogatives of investors. Though there are literally hundreds to choose from, an article she wrote on April 14, 1971, illustrates the point. On that day she reported that Campaign G.M., an organization of lawyers trying to force General Motors to accept candidates to its board of directors on petitions of shareholders and to permit employees, car dealers, and even customers to elect directors, had asked mutual funds to poll their shareholders on the issues. Campaign G.M. then asked the funds, Shanahan wrote, to vote their General Motors shares according to their shareholders' wishes. It was the first time that any attempt had been made to persuade mutual funds, banks, pension plans, and other big money managers, whose executives are as imperious as any Wall Streeter, to consider the wishes of their own shareholders. Partly because of the Shanahan stories, the issue grew to major proportions in 1971. The Shanahan article was typical of those she has written time and again in the public interest; her effectiveness, as we have seen, earned her a place on the Stock Exchange list of "unfriendlies."

Others at the *Times* have displayed concern for the investing public. A *New York Times* financial columnist, Bob Metz, occasionally shouldered arms in defense of the small investor. But though the personal feelings of some of its reporters to the contrary, the financial section of the *Times* has been written and edited to reflect the interests of Wall Street—in tune with the policy, apparently, of its editor, Tom Mullaney. This policy makes the financial section of a newspaper that is generally edited in the public interest seem like a business service edited for Wall Street. Indeed, the *Times'* pages have sometimes seemed an extension of the Exchange's promotional efforts. Typically, the financial pages of the *Times* will carry earnings reports, executive promotions, hard-to-understand articles on the economy, and the daily story of the stock market. Invariably, articles are written from management's point of view, since management and their spokesmen are the prime sources for the *Times'* financial reporters.

Basic issues, such as the way managements ignore stockholders wishes, get little play. In contrast, in May, 1970, when the newspaper's stock market reporter, Terry Robards, wrote a profile of Bernard J. Lasker, the Exchange chairman at the time, Lasker emerged a fearless leader, working to defend a revered institution (the Exchange) from attacks. Lasker, of course, was one of the insiders and specialists whose position gives them unusual power and wealth and who have been the subject of innumerable complaints and investigations by the SEC.

The policy of the *Times'* financial page editor, it must be said, does not prop up just the Street. Bank stories are written for banks by a reporter named Erich Heinemann, who writes stories few but bankers can understand much less see the need for. For example, in an April, 1971, story Heinemann titillated readers by hinting at the identity of the new economist about to be employed by the St. Louis Federal Reserve Bank. In other sections of the *Times* during recent years, an oil reporter named William Smith rode the oil tanker *Manhattan* to the Arctic where it had been sent by Humble Oil to determine the practicality and profitability of transporting oil by tanker from Alaska's North Slope. Smith sent back daily stories —and thereby lent the prestige of the *Times* to one of Humble's most successful promotions. In his accounts of perilous, crushing ice there was very little suggesting the peril to the ecology of 500,000-ton oil tankers breaking up in Arctic gales and spilling their cargoes into the sea.

Even the weekly column of the financial section's editor, Tom Mullaney, lends itself to the promotions of Wall Street. As it appears each Sunday, it is a summary of action in the stock market for the week and the influences, for example, a reported change in industrial production, that made the market act as it did. As a service to investors, it only tells them what they already know. As a service to Wall Street, it is a marvelous aid to keeping up investor interest and a highly regarded extension of editorial promotion.

Though the Street has been fertile with stories that would have swelled to the surface by dint of investigative reporting, the *Times* financial section has simply followed in the wake of events. Indeed, one day as the Exchange's Eugene Miller was sitting in his office with an associate, a telephone call inter- rupted their conversation. On the other end of Miller's line was a *Times* reporter. As Miller listened, his face creased into a smile of amusement, for the reporter was complaining that the Exchange was giving the *Wall Street Journal* more infor- mation than it was giving the *Times*.

It was a pathetic call for any reporter to make. In this case it was all the more pathetic for the simple fact was that the reporter was being beaten. The *Wall Street Journal* had been digging into Wall Street and the Stock Exchange in the best traditions of investigative reporting. From its editorial offices around the corner from the Stock Exchange, the *Journal* re- ported the troubles of the Street day after day in the late 1960s and early 1970s. There were the horror tales of the back office crushes, as well as the incompetence and dishon- esty of the firms. There was story after story detailing the insolvencies and others explaining the real reasons behind the Exchange's quest for higher commission rates. To be sure, the *Journal* never displayed much outrage on its editorial page to accompany the well-documented articles. The *Journal* is, after all, basically an industry trade publication that owes its livelihood to the Street, and its editorial writers much prefer to flog the government. But the *accounts* were there in all their gory detail, to be read by anyone and used to draw conclusions.

A number of able newsmen are involved in the *Journal's* sustained reporting effort, including such highly regarded professionals as Charles Stabler and Dave McClintick. Each did major roundups that added to the perspectives of their readers. The *Journal* reporter responsible for day-to-day coverage is Richard Rustin, a young man who acts the hard-nosed reporter to the point that it seems a put-on. Like his bosses, the editors of the *Journal,* Rustin shows little outrage or concern for the small investor in his copy. But his catalog of Wall Street's wrongdoing keeps the Stock Exchange upset and unhappy. Though Rustin is considered an "unfriendly," the Exchange dares not exclude him, say, from a small luncheon for the press, as it might exclude the reporter for the *New York Post.* His sources are so well placed and at so high a level that decisions made among top management of the Exchange on one day often appear in the *Journal* the next. Proposals barely ready for secret consideration by the board of governors at their Thursday meeting appear in print on Thursday morning—or even on Wednesday.

Indeed, secrets are leaked so often that Miller has introduced coded paper for recording highly confidential information. Whatever information is prepared on the special paper may not be seen even by most of the senior staff, not even by the confidential secretaries of the men who are authorized to view it. The coded paper has made little difference, however. It has served only to keep many of the senior staff in greater ignorance than before, thereby cutting into their effectiveness. Finally, it has been concluded that the leaks actually occur at the board of governors level.

For Rustin, the frustrations of Miller and the public relations staff are an enjoyable spectacle, and like many a reporter he practices a kind of petty tyranny. Frequently, he calls a public relations man five minutes before noon, suggesting lunch and causing the man to break already made appointments. A constant guest of Exchange public relations men at ball games and dinners, he refuses to write for the Exchange's publications on a free lance basis, pleading conflict of interest.

Still more serious than Rustin's flagellation, says one Street executive, and perhaps his most dangerous stories were those he wrote from the apparent conviction that Hayden, Stone, a firm eventually acquired by Cogan, Berlind, Weill & Levitt, would fail. It is this man's opinion that Rustin and the *Journal* helped bring Hayden, Stone down. "He raised the specter in 1969 of a major investment house folding. About a week later, Drew Pearson's column had a story much like Rustin's. At the time, Hayden, Stone was in serious trouble, but its failure was far from certain. If you want a bank, for instance, to fail or if you want to cause a run on it, get the news out to its depositors, who will then take their money out and cause the run to accelerate. The same can be done with an investment house in Wall Street, and this is what happened. The reporting of Rustin, especially in the case of Hayden, Stone, was quite obvious in its effect."

The point this man makes, that the press can create a panic, is a real one. But it is also open to argument. No one in the press *caused* Hayden, Stone's troubles and near-insolvency. Further, if both its investors and its customers, who were taking very real risks, did not already know of the firm's financial troubles, they certainly had a right to know. The sin, if there was one, was committed by the Hayden, Stone management.

It would be far more valid to criticize the press for its *lack* of coverage in Wall Street, rather than fault the un-bounded zeal of a Shanahan and Rustin or the sharpshooting of a Rossant. U.S. newspapers, news magazines, and the electronic press alike have been Wall Street's dupes for years since each has been euchred into presenting news of Wall Street that actually promotes the Street's main business: selling stocks.

It is gratuitous meaninglessness for television's newscasters, for example, to deliver reports of the movements of various stock averages. The figures tell most viewers nothing, but they do serve as a five or ten second promotion of the stock market. At the same time, stock movement, by and large, has been the extent of the efforts of television and radio newsmen to cover the market—though these same newsmen will devote a great deal of time to the sprained wrist of an outfielder. Occasionally, television newsmen have produced a documentary of the Street's ills, but only after the facts of Wall Street's behavior became so well known that they became impossible to ignore. One of the major promotional victories of the Exchange was to persuade some television stations to install a boardroom in their studios and to report market transactions minute by minute.

The major news magazines, compared with television, have done a far better job of exposing Wall Street, but they, too, have done little investigative reporting and, in fact, have been unmistakably followers, not leaders, as news gatherers. Their role, generally, has been that of assimilators of already known facts. It was not until late in April, 1971, for example, that *Time* magazine reported that the combination of negotiated commissions for large stock trades and a computerized stock market, a prototype of which exists in the over-the-counter market, could spell death for the Stock Exchange—and the end of the stock market for small investors. The possibilities had been explored weeks and weeks before in *Barron's*, a weekly sister publication of the *Wall Street Journal*, and by the *Institutional Investor*, a trade magazine that had raised the point as early as June, 1970. It was a *Time* financial editor, too—Purcell—who several years ago was let out of his job for payments from Wall Streeters in return for favorable articles. Though the weekly news magazines followed in the wake of smaller publications, their major roundups and large circulations were the chief reasons why many investors learned at least something—if belatedly—about the Street's incompetent, corrupt, and self-serving ways.

Few U.S. newspapers do much digging into Wall Street. The *Washington Post* has raised its voice occasionally. Most, however, faithfully reproduce the vast array of trivia and non-news sent them as handouts by the Stock Exchange and member firms or developed by their news services. The story of the *Manhattan*, for example, was picked up from the press release sent out by Humble Oil, almost word for word, and run as a feature story in the *Chicago Sun-Times* Sunday supplement, *Midwest* magazine. What should be filler copy often appears as featured news stories—for example, an estimate of dividends corporations will be paying in the year 2000. The daily stock tables, too, are an Exchange victory since they are nothing less than an advertisement for the Exchange's products and prices. Other advertisers of other products, such as the local department store, *pay* to have their ads published.

The reasons for the newspapers' dereliction have varied. To many publications, the Exchange looks like a respectable and truthful source. Wasn't it mandated by Congress to operate in the public interest? For many publishers, there is also an unwillingness to spend money on news gathering. Then there is the ignorance and the indifference of reporters, many of whom do not know and prefer not to know the difference between a stock and a bond although the economic well-being of many an American is tied irrevocably to one or the other or to both (in 1971 forty-one million people in the United States owned stocks).

Many a publisher also has found a golden opportunity in reporting on Wall Street to make money since investors are suckers for publications concerned with stocks. The huge rise of the *Wall Street Journal*'s circulation to over 1 million was not the result of offering the public matchless prose; it reflected a need among investors for the kind of boiler plate information that appears in the *Journal*. *Forbes* magazine, which analyzes stocks, industries, and the market itself, rose sharply to over 600,000 circulation for much the same reason. Investors also buy a host of other minor investment publications such as *Barrons*—most of which give them poor advice.

The Exchange has moved with great alacrity into the vacuum created by newspaper editors who were naive, lazy, and without publishers' support. Over the past twenty years it has produced an overwhelming volume of press releases, booklets, films, and even school curricula, all developed and written to make it easy for editors to drop them into their pages. The result is that most publications in the United States, barring only a few, offer themselves as supplements to the marketing programs of Wall Street.

In the course of things, columnists have sprung up, and as might be expected they are the darlings of the Stock Exchange since nearly all of them promote investment. Sam Shulsky, for example, a syndicated columnist who honestly tries to advise people on how to invest their money prudently, has favorite son status at the Stock Exchange. Another columnist, Sylvia Porter, does not give the precise kind of advice Shulsky distributes—her column does not generally discuss the merits of different stocks—but nevertheless she is so highly regarded that she merely has to request a special research project and the Exchange's research department will crank it into its work load and give the results to her on an exclusive basis.

A self-professed champion of the small investor, Sylvia Porter regarded the rise of the mutual fund, which poured money into brokers' coffers in huge amounts for years, as a blessing for the small investor. All during the 1950s and the 1960s she spread the Exchange's theory that mutual funds and other institutions would be stabilizing forces in the stock market, though they had been feared by SEC economists as far back as the 1930s. As responsible money managers, she said, the funds "would invest with care for the long term and thus would tend to push up prices and narrow price changes."

It is not known when the disillusionment set in. There may have been no disillusionment at all, in fact, only a feeling of uncomfortableness in the face of facts that had been clear for years. Whatever made her do it, in May, 1970, Sylvia Porter apologized publicly to her investor readers, saying she "couldn't anticipate—nor could you—that respected, trusted professional managers of money would become so emotional and erratic they would actually threaten the liquidity of America's great stock markets for the first time in history." The columnist, who was obviously still pro-stock Exchange, was referring to the fact that mutual fund managers and even some gentle college professors in charge of endowments were actually "go-go" when it came to putting big chunks of money into the market. They were not *investors,* as Sylvia Porter had led her readers to believe for twenty years, but the biggest *traders* in the stock market's history. "They have strained the very machinery of the organized stocks markets," she said, outraged, and she "condemned" them.

Equally effective as the vast array of information disseminated by the Exchange in winning over columnists and the press is the cozy relationship Wall Street has established with the press. Relations are so cozy, in fact, that members of the financial press stage the *Financial Follies,* a musical show of sorts in which the actors—reporters and writers—ostensibly lampoon major financial figures but, in fact, denigrate the performers since the show appears a base currying of favor. The *Follies* is merely a single episode in Wall Street's courting—and winning—of the financial press. The efforts of the Exchange staff, led by former *Fortune* magazine writer George Bookman continue all year long. Bookman's staff literally wines and dines reporters at lunch and dinner and generously buy admissions to important occasions for reporters whose publications will not themselves pay for tickets. The staff also takes reporters to baseball games and to expensive restaurants for dinner, as Bookman himself did when he took the *Journal's* Rustin to New York's Voison. For years the Exchange even conducted an annual golf outing to generate a cameraderie among reporters and top-level Exchange management—and to ply the reporters with food and drink. It is hard to say how many heads were turned upon meeting some of the most powerful and influential men in America at the golf outings, but those who were unfriendly to the Exchange were not invited again. Significantly, attendance at the tournament rose year by year. The sequel to the golf outing used to be the Exchange's annual Christmas party—an event canceled by Haack in favor of a lavish, but more exclusive, Christmas luncheon.

While it lasted, the Exchange's Christmas party was a legend. Most Street reporters remember it with fondness even today, for it was regarded by most of them as the most opulent "bash" put on anywhere. The party also had its desired effect. After it was over it was generally hard to find an anti-Wall Street reporter anywhere willing to blow the whistle.

Some years ago the sports side of newspaper editorial departments was called the kindergarten. Today's financial press may be an even more juvenile group. While millions upon millions of Americans have become involved in the market, putting their savings into stocks, the Street has been allowed to work under wraps. The press, to be sure, has done more to expose Wall Street's dark side than any other agency—to the shame of the SEC, law enforcement agencies, and even the Congress. But the work has been done by only a few men and women, and the Exchange has been able to remain a private club, keeping its members' anti-public ways unknown to the small investor simply because so many of the press are not doing their jobs. It is time that the financial press got to work.

Part 5

Conclusions

16

The reforms that are needed

THE time clearly has come to strip Wall Street
of its monopoly and its self-regulatory privilege—a privilege
that it has abused to benefit a few—and to change the securities
trading industry into one that is comprehensively regulated, as
are airlines and utilities.

The evidence showing that such reforms are needed is
overwhelming. All the power that the New York Stock Exchange exercises as a regulator should be placed with the SEC
by act of Congress, a move that was blocked by Wall Street
when Congress passed the Securities Act of 1934. Ways should
also be found to give SEC chairmen and commissioners far
more authority and freedom to act independently. Congress
needs also to examine more critically the candidates nominated
for SEC chairmanships, for in the past those candidates have
frequently been nothing more than the tools of Wall Street.
A few SEC chairmen have used the office to propel themselves
ahead personally, while others, though starting out with good

intentions, have become so fearful of the power Wall Street can bring to bear that they have been intimidated into silence.

In the future, the Exchange should be encouraged, even forced, to play a key role in the development of a national, truly free stock market, held together not by Exchange members but by an electronic network of computers, wire services, and electronic screens. There is no longer any practical reason, considering modern telecommunications systems, to make the corner of Broad and Wall Streets in New York the site of the biggest market for auctioning the stocks of the biggest corporations in the world—with prices determined by one man whose resources and ethics may prove inadequate to the task. The rise of the third market, in which independent firms trade competitively in Exchange-listed stocks, suggests a new era; so does the rise of direct trading between institutions in the "fourth market." Even the increased trading in regional exchanges suggests the need for a truly national stock market.

What is needed is a vast telecommunications network, modeled perhaps after the one adopted in February, 1971, in the over-the-counter market. Called NASDAQ (National Association of Securities Dealers Automatic Quotation), the system's hardware consists of a central computer, electronic screens much like television screens, and sending and receiving equipment. The importance of NASDAQ is that it provides the basis for a truly competitive auction market with market-making done in the open (or at least through subscribers' electronic screens), not secretly in the notebook of a mysterious figure on the floor of the Stock Exchange who acts for himself 30 percent of the time. Market-makers who subscribe to NASDAQ merely enter their bid and ask prices into a central computer's memory bank. By punching the proper sequence of buttons, other subscribers—brokers and dealers—can find out in seconds the bid and ask prices quoted by *all* those firms making a market in a stock. Then the broker can accept the best price available. In such a system the Exchange's specialist would wield no more power than other market-makers throughout the United States and even the world.

Though, it, too, would need comprehensive supervision—
just a few weeks after NASDAQ's startup its dealer-subscribers
were found to be reneging on the quotes they had put into the
system—a NASDAQ-like stock market could well be the salva-
tion of the true auction market; with a national electronic
system, a market for buying and selling by individual investors
could be maintained, and the huge numbers of investors would
insure the liquidity the Exchange has advocated over the years.
Such a vast and liquid stock market would be able to absorb
the huge blocks of stock traded by institutions not, as is today
necessary, on a negotiated basis in secret and at prices better
than the average investor can get but on an open, public-
auction basis. Truly huge blocks might have to be split up for
trading purposes, but this would be a problem of arithmetic
not of liquidity.

A national auction market would attract thousands of firms
who would welcome individual investors since the cost of
handling their accounts would be reduced. And as a corollary,
the growth in investment opportunities would tend to limit
the growth of mutual funds and other institutions, such as
banks, pension funds, and insurance companies, that are wield-
ing a disproportionate amount of economic power. Indeed, the
institutions—nearly all of them—have demonstrated that they,
too, need to be supervised and controlled far more closely
than is now the case. Mutual funds, for example, have exercised their economic power over Wall Street to reduce commissions and gain large discounts but with no assurance that
such savings will be passed on to their shareholders. On the
contrary, there is reason to believe that the fund managers are
the beneficiaries. At the same time, the funds have failed to
reflect the wishes of their shareholders in voting the stock they
hold beneficially for those shareholders. They have not re-
frained, however, from engaging in shady deals. The SEC's
study of institutional investors shows that many a mutual
fund secretly has helped one corporation take over another
by buying up big blocks of stock in a target company and
then holding those blocks until the acquiring company has

made a public offer to shareholders of the target company. With a fund's block of shares in its pocket, the acquiring company has fewer shares to round up, and its takeover is made that much easier. As for the fund, it profits from the collusion by selling its block for the tender price, which is usually higher than the price it paid originally for the shares.

The investment record of the mutual funds, even of college endowment funds, pension funds, and all the rest of the go-go money managers is nothing to crow about, either. At least one authoritative study, conducted by Irwin Friend of the Wharton School of the University of Pennsylvania and two associates, Jean Crockett and Marshall Blume, called *Mutual Funds and Other Institutional Investors: A New Perspective* and published by the 20th Century Fund, has shown that institutions performed no better in the bull markets of the late 1960s than did all the issues on the Exchange taken together. High-risk funds, in fact, performed worse than the averages of Standard & Poor's Composite Index.

Any number of statistical studies show that in the bear market of 1969 and 1970 the funds lost money at enormous rates. Some lost 25 percent or more of their assets. Yet professional management in the marketplace is all that the funds are really selling to their shareholders. Indeed, that is all any of the institutions—banks, pension plans, savings investment plans of corporations, endowment funds—have to offer the people whose money they are managing.

But poor performance does not mean that the money managers themselves will not get rich. Take the mutual funds. For years they have charged buyers of their shares a front-end load of 8 percent, sometimes more, taking this percentage of an individual's investment for themselves before issuing him any shares or doing any work for him. On top of this, they also levy a management fee ranging from .0625 to .5 percent on the net assets of the fund, paying it to themselves through dummy management companies. Some funds controlled by brokers, for instance Lehman Brothers, which owns the One William Street Fund, even execute trades through the brokerage side of their business. Thus in 1969, Lehman Brothers, while collecting over $900,000 for advising the One William Street Fund, also received $640,000 from the fund in commissions.

Some funds such as Investors Diversified Services even insist that the assets of the fund be used to indemnify officers and directors for expenses that may be incurred in defending themselves against legal actions. Though the SEC has advised IDS that indemnification is against public policy as expressed in the Securities Act of 1933, IDS has decided, nevertheless, to oppose the SEC in court. Indemnification costs could be no small thing, for the funds are being sued on many counts. IDS, for example, is a defendant in a suit charging that Glenn Alden Corporation sold 92,700 shares of Schenley Industries to IDS at a price $1.5 million below the true value. IDS is also a defendant in a case charging civil violation of the antitrust laws, violations of the Investment Company Act of 1940 (passed by Congress expressly to regulate mutual funds) with respect to giveups, and for participating in reciprocal business with brokers.

It is obvious that among many needed reforms in the securities markets, subjecting the funds to far tighter controls should take high priority. Fund assets, for example, should not be allowed to rise beyond $50 million. In this way the economic muscle they exert can be curbed. Fund managers must also be strictly limited in their trading activities and required to hold the shares they purchase for a minimum period of time. Studies suggest that this might well improve their performance in the market and at the same time reduce the chaotic conditions caused by their in-and-out activity. No broker should be permitted to manage a fund, either. It is far too tempting for a fund manager to churn his portfolio, knowing that he or his firm will be the beneficiary of the commissions generated. The charges levied upon fund share buyers are also too high. Not only should front-end loads be outlawed but the management fees, levied whether the fund performs well or not, should be eliminated. Many an independent investment counselor charges his clients on the basis of gains, and the funds ought to conform to the same principle. The misuse of share-holders' assets should also be subject to strict laws with criminal penalties.

Of crucial importance to the investing public is the method of remunerating stock brokers. These "customers' men" must be put on salary, for income tied strictly to commissions tempts them to churn the accounts of their customers. If special rewards seem necessary, and the brokers' salesmen are frequently cast in the role of adviser by their customers, then a bonus for performance would be reasonable. As for the salesmen's bosses, there is an undeniable need for them to learn competent management techniques. Further, when customers entrust their securities and cash to brokers for safekeeping, it must be made law that these assets cannot be mingled with the firms' own securities and cash. Jail terms and fines should be imposed for the slightest infraction in this area. The loss of funds perhaps accumulated for retirement can destroy the security of an individual for life and create untold anguish. The time is long past due in the Street for meting out penalties commensurate with the seriousness of theft and misuse of customers' assets.

A call for such penalties means that the lawyers and prosecutors of the United States must become involved in the problem at a meaningful level. Too many lawyers are connected too tightly to Wall Street, and too many of the more prestigious law firms have sought money instead of justice, thus turning their backs on the wrongdoings of the exchanges, their member firms, and the stock brokers.

But if lawyers have failed to blow the whistle, the press has failed even more dramatically. Editors everywhere need to take a look at the people in their financial editorial departments and determine whether the reporters and department editors have divided interests. Editors must determine whether or not their people are flacks for Wall Street, ready and willing to go on junkets and accept favors. During a newspaper strike in New York during the 1960s many a financial reporter was hired by the Stock Exchange, thereby creating a conflict of interest for the reporter. When he returned to his publication he could not possibly cover his Wall Street beat with objectivity. Yet those same reporters still write for their newspapers.

It is from the reporters, the editors, the lawyers, and the Congress that reform in Wall Street, so badly needed, must come. True, the marketplace itself is becoming more competitive and the monopoly of the Exchange is tending to slip away. But the Exchange still has enormous power, and though changes might be coming in the way securities are traded, most of the men in Wall Street—the same ones who have perpetrated wrongs for years—are maneuvering to stay on top. In the changes being suggested for Wall Street by William McChesney Martin, emphasis has been put on changing the system. But the Martin recommendations would let Wall Street continue to regulate itself and to fix commission rates. Self-regulation is the heart of Wall Street's power, while high minimum commission rates are the means by which inefficient, corrupt firms have been able to maintain themselves. As Martin must know, since once before he introduced reform to Wall Street, new reform that continues these two powers will be corrupted! What needs to be emphasized, through enforcement of new, tough laws, is that the men involved in Wall Street's variety of chicanery face certain punishment. What they need to understand is that the investing public will be abused no longer.

Index

240